D1712598

S.E. Hinton

WHO
WROTE
THAT?

WHO WROTE THAT?

S.E. Hinton

Dennis Abrams

**Foreword by
Kyle Zimmer**

CHELSEA HOUSE
PUBLISHERS
An imprint of Infobase Publishing

S.E. Hinton

Copyright © 2009 by Infobase Publishing

Chelsea House
An imprint of Infobase Publishing
132 West 31st Street
New York NY 10001

Library of Congress Cataloging-in-Publication Data
Abrams, Dennis, 1960-
S.E. Hinton / Dennis Abrams.
p. cm. — (Who wrote that?)
Includes bibliographical references and index.
ISBN 978-1-60413-088-1
1. Hinton, S.E.—Criticism and interpretation. 2. Authors, American—
20th century—Biography—Juvenile literature. 3. Young adult fiction—Authorship—
History and criticism. I. Title. II. Series.
PS3558.I548Z54 2009
813'.54—dc22
          2008035046

Chelsea House books are available at special discounts when purchased in bulk quantities for business, associations, institutions, or sales promotions. Please call our Special Sales Department in New York at (212) 967-8800 or (800) 322-8755.

You can find Chelsea House on the World Wide Web at http://www.chelseahouse.com

Text design by Keith Trego
Cover design by Jooyoung An and Alicia Post

Printed in the United States of America

Bang EJB 10 9 8 7 6 5 4 3 2 1

This book is printed on acid-free paper.

Table of Contents

FOREWORD BY
KYLE ZIMMER
PRESIDENT, FIRST BOOK

HUMANITY IS POWERED by stories. From our earliest days as thinking beings, we employed every available tool to tell each other stories. We danced, drew pictures on the walls of our caves, spoke, and sang. All of this extraordinary effort was designed to entertain, recount the news of the day, explain natural occurrences— and then gradually to build religious and cultural traditions and establish the common bonds and continuity that eventually formed civilizations. Stories are the most powerful force in the universe; they are the primary element that has distinguished our evolutionary path.

Our love of the story has not diminished with time. Enormous segments of societies are devoted to the art of storytelling. Book sales in the United States alone topped $24 billion in 2006; movie studios spend fortunes to create and promote stories; and the news industry is more pervasive in its presence than ever before.

There is no mystery to our fascination. Great stories are magic. They can introduce us to new cultures, or remind us of the nobility and failures of our own, inspire us to greatness or scare us to death; but above all, stories provide human insight on a level that is unavailable through any other source. In fact, stories connect each of us to the rest of humanity not just in our own time, but also throughout history.

This special magic of books is the greatest treasure that we can hand down from generation to generation. In fact, that spark in a child that comes from books became the motivation for the creation of my organization, First Book, a national literacy program with a simple mission: to provide new books to the most disadvantaged children. At present, First Book has been at work in hundreds of communities for over a decade. Every year children in need receive millions of books through our organization and millions more are provided through dedicated literacy institutions across the United States and around the world. In addition, groups of people dedicate themselves tirelessly to working with children to share reading and stories in every imaginable setting from schools to the streets. Of course, this Herculean effort serves many important goals. Literacy translates to productivity and employability in life and many other valid and even essential elements. But at the heart of this movement are people who love stories, love to read, and want desperately to ensure that no one misses the wonderful possibilities that reading provides.

When thinking about the importance of books, there is an overwhelming urge to cite the literary devotion of great minds. Some have written of the magnitude of the importance of literature. Amy Lowell, an American poet, captured the concept when she said, "Books are more than books. They are the life, the very heart and core of ages past, the reason why men lived and worked and died, the essence and quintessence of their lives." Others have spoken of their personal obsession with books, as in Thomas Jefferson's simple statement: "I live for books." But more compelling, perhaps, is the almost instinctive excitement in children for books and stories.

Throughout my years at First Book, I have heard truly extraordinary stories about the power of books in the lives of children. In one case, a homeless child, who had been bounced from one location to another, later resurfaced— and the only possession that he had fought to keep was the book he was given as part of a First Book distribution months earlier. More recently, I met a child who, upon receiving the book he wanted, flashed a big smile and said, "This is my big chance!" These snapshots reveal the true power of books and stories to give hope and change lives.

As these children grow up and continue to develop their love of reading, they will owe a profound debt to those volunteers who reached out to them—a debt that they may repay by reaching out to spark the next generation of readers. But there is a greater debt owed by all of us—a debt to the storytellers, the authors, who have bound us together, inspired our leaders, fueled our civilizations, and helped us put our children to sleep with their heads full of images and ideas.

Who Wrote That? is a series of books dedicated to introducing us to a few of these incredible individuals. While we have almost always honored stories, we have not uniformly honored storytellers. In fact, some of the most important authors have toiled in complete obscurity throughout their lives or have been openly persecuted for the uncomfortable truths that they have laid before us. When confronted with the magnitude of their written work or perhaps the daily grind of our own, we can forget that writers are people. They struggle through the same daily indignities and dental appointments, and they experience the intense joy and bottomless despair that many of us do. Yet somehow they rise above it all to deliver a powerful thread that connects us all. It is a rare honor to have the opportunity that these books provide to share the lives of these extraordinary people. Enjoy.

Above, a plaque and photo of the writer S.E. Hinton at her alma mater, Will Rogers High School in Tulsa, Oklahoma. Hinton was just a teenager when she wrote and published her first novel, **The Outsiders.**

1

Creating
Something New

IMAGINE FOR JUST a moment that it is 1965, 1966, or 1967. You're at the school library, the public library, or a bookstore, and you're looking for something to read. You want to find a novel with characters you can relate to, whose thoughts, feelings, and experiences speak to you and what you're thinking, feeling, and experiencing in your own life. What would your choices have been?

There were, of course, the tried and true classics, the kind of books your parents, grandparents, and even your great-grandparents might have read: Charles Dickens's *Oliver Twist*, Alexandre Dumas's *The Count of Monte Cristo*, Mark Twain's

The Adventures of Tom Sawyer, Louisa May Alcott's *Little Women*, or Rudyard Kipling's *The Jungle Book*. Though none of these books had been written specifically for a young adult audience, over the years they became the kind of classics that were considered "good for kids to read." Although all of these books are highly enjoyable and well worth reading, they don't speak directly to the concerns and experiences of the contemporary young reader.

There were other books available as well—more contemporary titles that were also considered "worthy" of a young reader's time—books such as *My Friend Flicka*, about a boy and his horse; *Johnny Tremain*, the story of an apprentice silversmith in the days leading up to the American Revolutionary War; and *Anne of Green Gables*, which grew into an entire series of books relating the life of a young orphan raised on Canada's Prince Edward Island. There were also newer award-winning books, such as E.L. Konigsburg's *From the Mixed-up Files of Mrs. Basil E. Frankweiler* (1967), about a brother and sister who run away to New York City's Metropolitan Museum of Art to teach their parents a lesson, and *The Black Pearl* (1967), which tells of the coming of age of the son of a pearl dealer in Baja, California. These were all excellent books, but they were the kind of books that parents and librarians *wanted* you to read. Again, they did not come close to exploring the emotional reality of being a young adult.

There were also contemporary books available that had been written for an adult audience, but were later embraced by younger audiences. These include J.D. Salinger's *A Catcher in the Rye* and William Golding's *Lord of the Flies*, both of which struck chords with young adult readers. Both are great, classic books for young adults, but can average teenage readers, dealing with issues such as school violence, drugs, dating, and trying to belong, find in these books anything relevant to their lives?

Even books written during that period aimed specifically at young adult readers often missed the mark. Written by adults who were looking back at their own childhoods, they tended to see young adulthood as a golden period, where the worst problems anyone faced were whether or not Bobby would make the team or the school quarterback would realize he liked Cheryl in time to invite her to the school dance.

For example, in Beverly Cleary's *Fifteen*, the novel's plot centers around high school sophomore Jane Purdy's experiences dating upperclassman Stan Crandall. First written and published in the 1950s, *Fifteen* reflects a time when a couple would often go on several dates and agree to go steady before they would even think about holding hands or sharing their first kiss. Although to many the book describes an ideal teen romance, for most teens in the mid-1960s (and perhaps even more so today), the characters in *Fifteen* could seem as remote as Tom Sawyer or Oliver Twist.

For one young woman growing up in Tulsa, Oklahoma, the situation was particularly frustrating. As a junior in high school, Susan Eloise Hinton loved to read but could find nothing available that bore any resemblance to the life she was living. To remedy the situation, she decided to write a book herself. As she said in an interview with Teresa Miller that was published in Hinton's short story collection, *Some of Tim's Stories*, "If you were through the animal books and you weren't ready for an adult book, there was nothing to read except *Mary Jane Goes to the Prom* and *Tommy Hits a*

Home Run. I couldn't find anything that dealt with teenage life as I was seeing it, so in one sense I wrote it just to have something to read."[1]

In 1965, Hinton sat down at her father's old Underwood typewriter and started work on a novel that would fully and accurately describe the teenage world she knew: The story told of Ponyboy, his brothers, and their friends; their constant struggle to belong; and the conflicts between the haves and the have-nots. Two years later, the completed novel, *The Outsiders*, was published to nearly universal praise. Susan Eloise Hinton, now known to the world as S.E. Hinton, made publishing history by single-handedly creating a new genre of fiction—the young adult novel.

Did you know...

Many readers find religious symbolism in *The Outsiders*. According to S.E. Hinton, many of her fans claim that the character Johnny Cade is a Jesus figure who dies saving people. Not only does he "come back" from the dead with his final message for Ponyboy, but his death also takes place between the deaths of the two criminals, Dallas and Bob. When he goes to buy groceries, Johnny writes in the dust on the ground "Be back soon," signing it "J.C." Hinton says that any religious symbolism in the book was not put there consciously and that she feels a great deal of her writing is, in fact, subconscious.

With estimated total sales of more than 14 million copies to date, *The Outsiders* changed the face of publishing. As John Daly said in his study *Presenting S.E. Hinton*, "*The Outsiders* has become the most successful, and the most emulated, young adult book of all time."[2]

The Outsiders remains Hinton's most popular and most beloved book. With her first book, Hinton struck a chord with her readers that continues to reverberate today. As she said in an interview with *Vanity Fair* in 2007, "I get the same letters from *Outsiders* readers as I did 40 years ago. And it's selling as well today as it ever has. The kids still identify with the emotions, the social injustice. The uniforms change, the names change, but the groups go on forever. And now I am getting letters from parents who say it was their favorite book, and they're sharing it with their kids."[3]

Thanks to S.E. Hinton, readers now have an overwhelming abundance of young adult novels from which to choose. Since the publication of *The Outsiders*, the topics available to the writers of young adult novels have become virtually limitless, and they are now free to explore nearly every aspect of what it means to be a teenager. Robert Cormier, Richard Peck, Gary Soto, M.E. Kerr, Paula Danziger, and many others have had the freedom to write the books that they wanted to write because of S.E. Hinton.

Judy Blume's groundbreaking novel, *Forever*, for instance, explores the topics of a teen's first sexual encounter and teen pregnancy—a world light-years away from Beverly Cleary's *Fifteen*. The Gossip Girl series, including *You're the One that I Want* and *Would I Lie to You*, describes the world of privileged teens at a New York private school. The 2007 Michael L. Printz winner for best young adult novel, *American Born Chinese*, uses the format of a graphic novel to follow a Chinese-American teenager's struggle to define himself against racial stereotypes. The "Bluford" series, including such titles as *Lost and Found* and *The Fallen*, illustrates what life is like in a fictional inner-city high school named for the first black astronaut. Laurie Hales Anderson's *Speak* tells the story of a ninth-grade girl who was raped.

Indeed, almost any controversial topic can be found in today's young adult fiction. James Blasingame, an Arizona State University professor who edits the *Assembly on Literature for Adolescents Review*, said, "There's something for everyone now. A lot of [young adult] authors said, 'When I was a teen, the book I needed was not there, so I wrote it.'" He went on to add, "Kids want books that reflect their real lives."[4]

Without S.E. Hinton to lead the way, though, today's world of young adult literature would be a very different place: It would lack the books that truly reflect the reality of the teenage experience. In her groundbreaking book, *The Outsiders*, as well as in her subsequent novels, *That Was Then, This Is Now*; *Rumble Fish*; *Tex*; and *Taming the Star Runner*, Hinton described for the first time the lives of young adults as they really are. By doing so, she opened the door for every other young adult writer who has followed.

Hinton's accomplishments are so important that when the Young Adult Library Services Association (YALSA), together with *School Library Journal* magazine, established the Margaret A. Edwards Award in 1988 to honor an author's lifetime achievement in writing books that have been popular with teenagers, its first award recipient was S.E. Hinton. As it says on the YALSA Web site,

Susan Eloise Hinton is the first recipient of the YASA/SLJ Author Achievement Award. This award was created to honor an author whose work has been taken to heart by young adults over a period of years, providing an "authentic voice that continues to illuminate their experiences and emotions, giving insight into their lives." S.E. Hinton's work is recognized as having the following: [a] lasting ability to speak to the young adult experience, to help readers become more aware of themselves and of the world around them. . . . the Young Adult Services Division recognizes that these books provide a window through which young adults can view their world. In them a young adult may explore the need for independence and simultaneously the need for loyalty and belonging, the need to care for others, and the need to be cared for by them.[5]

How did she do it? How did a shy, quiet girl from Tulsa, Oklahoma, write a book about teenage boys that changed the world of publishing forever? What were her inspirations? How did she follow her initial success? In other words, how did Susan Eloise Hinton become S.E. Hinton, one of the most influential and beloved authors of our time?

A photo of the Tulsa skyline on a cloudy day. All of Hinton's books are set in and around her native city, where she still lives.

2

Finding Her Voice

I was born in Tulsa, Oklahoma, where I have lived most of my life. There is nothing to do there, but it is a pleasant place to live if you don't want to do anything. . . .[1]

—S.E. Hinton

IT IS OFTEN the case that writers set their novels in or around the place of their birth. Many of William Faulkner's novels are set in Mississippi, in the mythical Yoknapatawpha County. His hometown, Oxford, is the county seat of Lafayette County, on which Yoknapatawpha County is based. A large number of John Steinbeck's works are set in Salinas County, California, the place of his birth. By rooting their work in a place they

19

know well, authors are able to give the reader a strong sense of place and time.

Hinton works the same way. All of her work is set in or around the place she knows best—the place of her birth and where she still lives today: Tulsa, Oklahoma. Even when the book does not say it takes place in Tulsa, it *is* in Tulsa. In *Tex*, for example, when Tex and Mason go to the "city," they are going to Tulsa. When Tex tells Cole Collins over a pay phone that "he's across from the big hotel that looks like a castle,"[2] he is describing a real hotel, the Camelot. (The Camelot was demolished in 2007 after being left vacant for more than 10 years.) The drive-in movie theater described in *The Outsiders* is the real-life Admiral Twin Drive-In. (The Admiral Twin Drive-In, with a capacity of more than 1,500 cars, still exists as Oklahoma's largest drive-in movie theater.) By using the places she knows so well in her books, Hinton is able to let the reader get to know them as well.

WHERE SHE COMES FROM

What ultimately became the City of Tulsa was originally part of Indian Territory and was first settled by the Loachapoka and Creek tribes in 1836. They established a home under an oak tree at the present-day intersection of Cheyenne Avenue and 18th Street, and named their new settlement "Tallasi," meaning "old town" in the Creek language, which later became "Tulsa."

In 1898, Tulsa was just a small town in northeastern Oklahoma. Three years later, Tulsa's first oil well, named Sue Bland No. 1, was established. By 1905, the discovery of additional oil prompted an explosion of growth and development: Tulsa's population grew from 1,390 in 1900 to more than 140,000 in 1930. Because of the city's success in the energy industry, Tulsa was known as the "Oil Capital of the World" for most of the twentieth century.

Along with the riches from the oil, however, came changes. The city's original inhabitants, many of whom were descendants of the area's original American Indian population, were joined by the "new rich," and Tulsa began to divide into neighborhoods based on money. The people with money moved into the residential southern and eastern sides of Tulsa, where they built large homes that reflected their economic status. The city's working- and middle-class families generally lived in north and west Tulsa. (The Arkansas River divides the city nearly down the middle.) The majority of these less-well-off families worked at blue-collar jobs in the oil refineries or at McDonnell Douglas plants in north Tulsa. It is this divided city that Hinton explored in *The Outsiders*.

CHILDHOOD

Although it is known that Susan Eloise Hinton was born in Tulsa, Oklahoma, there is some question as to her actual birth date. This confusion is due to the fact that because Hinton was so young when she wrote *The Outsiders* her editor at Viking Press, concerned that nobody would believe that someone so young could actually have written the book, added one or two years to her age. To this day, Hinton refuses to verify her exact age, but most sources agree that she was born on July 22, 1950.

Hinton's father, Grady Hinton, was a door-to-door salesman. Her mother, Lillian, worked on an assembly line. Hinton also has a younger sister, Beverly. For years, Hinton did not speak publicly about her childhood, saying only that it was a typical one involving family, friends, and pets. However, in an interview with the *New York Times* in 2005, she admitted for the first time, "My mother was physically and emotionally abusive. My father was an extremely cold man."[3]

Feeling distant and separate from her parents, Hinton did not find consolation in organized religion. In an interview with Teresa Miller in *Some of Tim's Stories* she said, "Early on I rejected organized religion. As a child, I went to a very fundamentalist church and saw a man preaching hell-fire and brimstone under a sign that said 'God is Love.' It turned me against organized religion for the rest of my life. It did not turn me against God. To me, organized religion is like organized social classes, based on exclusion. God is inclusive."[4]

She did, however, find comfort in visiting her grand-mother's farm. There, Hinton, the self-proclaimed tomboy, was able to ride horses and even dreamed of eventually becoming a cowboy—at least until she discovered how hard it was. Her grandmother's farm was also the place where Hinton found a retreat in the world of books and

Did you know...

Hinton's son Nick wants to have a career in film-sound engineering. He even did an internship at George Lucas' Skywalker Ranch and studied film-sound design. Hinton hopes her son is able to get into a field that he loves as much as she loves writing.

writing—and the means to escape what was obviously a hurtful family situation.

BOOKS AND FITTING IN

I always just plain liked to write, and I always liked to read. Part of the reason I started to write was to have something to read.[5]
—S.E. Hinton

A reader from an early age, the first book Hinton remembers taking out from the library was called *Peanuts the Pony*. Hinton wrote in the *Fourth Book of Junior Authors*,

> I started reading about the same time everyone else did, and began to write a short time later. The major influence on my writing has been my reading. I read everything, including Comet cans and coffee labels. Reading taught me sentence structure, paragraphing, how to build a chapter. Strangely enough, it never taught me spelling.
>
> I've always written about things that interest me, so my first years of writing (grade three through ten) I wrote about cowboys and horses. I wanted to be a cowboy and have a horse. I was strange for my era, but feel quite comfortable in this one, when everyone wants to be a cowboy and I have a horse.[6]

Indeed, many of the books that Hinton read when she was a girl were also about horses and other animals: *Duff, the Story of a Bear*; Marguerite Henry's horse books, *King of the Wind*; and Ernest Thompson Seton's *Wild Animals I Have Known* were among her favorites.

Of course, Hinton read about more than horses and cowboys. She was a big fan of Shirley Jackson's *The Haunting of Hill House*, and as anyone who has read *The Outsiders* would guess, she loved the novel *Gone with the Wind* by

Pictured above, a manual Underwood typewriter, similar to the one owned by Hinton's father on which she learned how to type. In ninth grade, she bred and sold puppies in order to buy her own Underwood.

Margaret Mitchell. She was, as she points out in an interview, a very eclectic reader, reading as many different kinds of books as she could get her hands on.

As much as she enjoyed many of the books she read, they still weren't telling her the kinds of stories that she wanted and needed to hear. To remedy this, she started writing herself, and by the time she was in third grade she was certain that she wanted to be a writer. As she said in an interview with Lisa Ehrichs in *Seventeen* magazine, "I started [writing] in grade school—it was just something I enjoyed doing. I was the type of girl who loved horses and cowboys, so I wrote about them. I read a lot and had fun making up my own stories."[7]

What did Hinton use to write her stories? Keep in mind that she was writing before computers came on the scene; even electric typewriters were a relatively new development. (IBM introduced its Selectric typewriter in 1961.) So, when Hinton sat down to write, she did so in front of a manual typewriter, meaning it had no electrical or any other outside source of power: Its power was derived solely from the typist's own fingers. As Hinton said in an interview, "My first typewriter. I taught myself to type on my dad's old Underwood, and I still have it. I must have had fingers of steel to type on that thing."[8]

Indeed, writing was so important to Hinton that when she was in ninth grade, she had her dog, a cocker spaniel, bred and then sold the puppies to earn the money to buy a typewriter of her very own. It was an Underwood, and a manual at that, but still, the new typewriter was easier for her to work on than her father's old one.

Although Hinton enjoyed making up her own stories, her family felt differently about it. The Hinton household, with the exception of Susan, was not interested in books and writing, did not understand Susan's need to write, and felt that she was cutting out her family by locking herself away to read and write. Her mother, in particular, did not understand her daughter's need to write. "When I was writing she'd come into my room, grab my hair, and throw me in front of the TV," Hinton told the *New York*

Times. "She'd say, 'You're part of this family—now act like it.' I hate TV now."[9] (It is interesting to note that in Hinton's novel *Taming the Star Runner*, the stepfather of the main character, Travis, throws his manuscripts into the fireplace and forces him to watch TV with the family when he would rather be in his room writing.)

Despite her family's objections, Hinton kept writing. "I would tell myself, 'It'll get better. Hang on.'"[10] She even managed to complete two novels (neither of which have been published) before entering high school. Hinton had no idea that she was about to enter a world that would give her the inspiration to write her first major novel.

WILL ROGERS HIGH SCHOOL

The mid-1960s, when Susan Hinton was in high school, was a period of remarkable and rapid social and political change. The struggle for equal rights for African Americans was in full swing. Protests erupted as the nation became deeply involved in the Vietnam War. Many women began challenging their traditional roles as stay-at-home wives and mothers.

On the other hand, although these events certainly made themselves felt in Tulsa, Oklahoma, life in many ways continued as it always had. As Marylou Morano Kjelle notes in her biography *S.E. Hinton*, the students at Will Rogers High School were not politically active, focusing instead on their studies, social lives, and after-school activities.

From today's perspective, it seems like a different world. The girls took dance lessons at Skilly's School of Ballroom Dancing and belonged to one of two dance sororities: the Damsels or the Highlanders. Boys had their own social club called the Vikings or pursued athletic activities during "sixth hour gym." Some boys belonged to the Order of DeMolay, an international Masonic organization that taught leadership skills to teenage boys.

Outside the organized after-school activities, the students of Will Rogers High School, like high school students everywhere and at every time, settled into their own social groups. The two most prominent groups were the "greasers," the children of working-class families, and the "Socs" (pronounced "soshes," for Socials), whose parents were wealthy and upper-class.

The two groups were easily identifiable. As Ponyboy describes his group, the greasers, in *The Outsiders*, "We wear our hair long and dress in blue jeans and T-shirts, or leave our shirttails out and wear leather jackets and tennis shoes or boots."[11] With their long hair slicked back, hence the term "greasers," and a cigarette dangling from their lips, the look was complete. The Socs, on the other hand, dressed nicely in madras shirts and slacks and drove Mustangs or Corvettes. The two groups hated each other with a passion—a passion that often erupted into violence.

Susan Hinton was never a member of either the social clubs or the gangs: She was a writer. Indeed, because she had no clear ties to either group, she found herself easily moving back and forth between the two. She grew up in a greaser neighborhood, but found herself in Soc classrooms. So, although she didn't belong to either group, she found herself having friends in both.

Given the fact that all of her books are written from a male perspective, it is not all that surprising that her friends were mostly boys. Hinton had always found her life and interests distant from that of most girls of the time. As she said in an interview with Teresa Miller, published in *Some of Tim's Stories*, "I wasn't really typical of the female culture at that time, because all girls wanted to do was rat their hair and outline their eyes in black. I didn't want a boyfriend with a hot car; I wanted my own car."[12]

She also discussed this feeling of difference in a 1983 interview with the *New York Times*, saying of girls' lives at the time that "it was such a passive society. Girls got their status from their boyfriends. They weren't interested in doing anything on their own. I didn't understand what they were talking about."[13]

This is not to say that Hinton didn't have a boyfriend—she did, and they dated once a week—but for the most part, her life revolved around school, her part-time jobs working in a bookstore and operating an elevator, and, of course and most importantly, her writing. As she told Teresa Miller, "Writing actually was my life as a high school student. I wasn't the kind of kid who had to be hanging out with people all the time. . . . I was very serious. I was not unhappy being alone."[14]

Though she may have been a loner, a big part of her talent as a writer was her ability to observe and respond to what was going on around her. She saw how the greasers were put down by the Socs and was strongly aware of the injustice of it. "I just felt being part of my peer group so strongly," she remarked in a 2007 interview on CNN. "I was immersed in teen culture, but not taken in by it."[15]

She was not taken in by it, but she was angered by what she saw. Her anger continued to grow until it spilled over onto the page, as she noted in *Seventeen* in 1967,

"I felt the greasers were getting knocked when they didn't deserve it. The custom, for instance, of driving by a shabby boy and screaming 'Greaser!" at him always made me boil. But it was the cold-blooded beating of a friend of mine that gave me the idea of writing a book; I wanted to do something that would change people's opinion of greasers."[16]

So, at the age of 15, when she was just a sophomore in high school, Susan Eloise Hinton began work on the book that would make her famous—*The Outsiders*.

WRITING *THE OUTSIDERS*

None of the events in the book [The Outsiders] *are taken from life, but the rest—how kids think and live and feel—is for real. The characters—Dallas, who wasn't tough enough; Sodapop, the happy-go-lucky drop out; Bob, the rich kid who didn't want to be a hood—they're all real to me, though I didn't put my friends into the book. The characters are mixtures of people I know, with a bit of myself thrown in.[17]*

—S.E. Hinton

Many people who aren't writers assume that a writer's first novel comes easily, that the words flow directly from the author to the page without a whole lot of thought and effort. That may be the case for some authors, but for Hinton, *The Outsiders* took one and a half years of serious effort. She wrote the first draft—40 single-spaced typewritten pages— without writing an outline and then continuously worked to revise her manuscript, as the characters and plot slowly revealed themselves to her.

During the time that she was working on the book, Hinton learned that her father, Grady, was suffering from a brain tumor. While he spent more and more time in the hospital, with his wife at his side, Hinton poured her emotions and grief into her manuscript. She worked on it at school. She wrote it on her family's kitchen table during the evening. Like any writer, she kept trying to improve her work, adding flashbacks, fleshing out the details, doing everything she could to make it better, to make it more *real*.

Through all these changes, the one thing that never wavered was her ultimate reason for writing the book. In a 1967 *New York Times* article entitled "Teen-Agers Are for Real," Hinton wrote about what was lacking in young adult literature, and what she hoped to provide:

> The trouble is, grown-ups write about teen-agers from their own memories, or else write about teen-agers from a stand-off, I'm-a-little-scared-to-get-close-they're-hairy view. Teen-agers today want to read about teen-agers today. The world is changing, yet the authors of books for teen-agers are still 15 years behind the times.
>
> In the fiction they write, romance is still the most popular theme, with a-horse-and-the-girl-who-loved-it coming in a close second. Nowhere is the drive-in social jungle mentioned, the behind-the-scenes politicking that goes on in big schools, the cruel social system in which, if you can afford to snub every fourth person you meet, you're popular. In short, where's reality?[18]

Reality was on the pages of her manuscript, which was completed her junior year of high school, around the same time her father passed away. Hinton was devastated by the loss but, at the same time, was proud of the book she had written. Although she had originally started the book out of her own need to write, she found herself wondering whether anyone else might enjoy reading it. How could an unpublished teenage writer from Tulsa, Oklahoma, get her book into the hands of a publisher?

A photo of the cast of The Outsiders, *a film directed by Francis Ford Coppola and based on Hinton's enormously popular first novel. From left: Emilio Esteves, Rob Lowe, C. Thomas Howell, Patrick Swayze, and Tom Cruise.*

Becoming Famous

HINTON KNEW HER book was good and started to let others read what she had written. (She had also taken advice from friends when she was writing the book. If she got stuck on plot, she'd go to school and tell people what had happened so far and then ask them what they thought should happen next.) After the mother of one of her friends read the manuscript, she sent it to a friend who was also a professional writer. This writer put Hinton in touch with her agent, Marilyn Marlow, at Curtis Brown Ltd. Hinton sent Marlow a copy of the manuscript, along with a letter, reprinted in *Some of Tim's Stories*, which said, "I started this book about three years ago as a short story, but I soon found that I couldn't get all I wanted to say into a short story. It was started for fun, but it means more to me than that."[1]

Interestingly, it was Hinton's younger sister, Beverly, who pushed her to send the manuscript to Marlow. Hinton had been talking with her mother about the book and wanted to know if she could buy herself a car if her book sold. Her mother disbelievingly told her that yes, if the book was sold she could get a car. Her sister heard the conversation and pushed her to get it in the mail. According to Hinton, her sister walked around for years afterward, saying, "I sent the book off. I sent the book off," to which Hinton replied, "Yeah, and you put the first dent in the car, too."[2]

Marlow *was* interested in the book, telling Hinton that she had "caught a certain spirit." The book sold to Viking Press, the second publisher that saw it. On the day she graduated from high school, Hinton received her first publishing contract, which offered her $1,000 to publish *The Outsiders*. Ironically, the soon-to-be-published author received a "D" in her creative writing class—she had spent so much time working on her book that she had neglected her work for class!

The young author also now had a pen name—the name under which her book would be published. Susan Eloise Hinton became S.E. Hinton. Why the name change? Her editor at Viking Press felt that since the protagonist of her book was male, it would be more believable if it appeared that a woman hadn't written the book. Hinton herself agreed with this line of thinking, telling *Seventeen*, "*The Outsiders*, like most of the things that I write, is written from a boy's point of view. That's why I'm listed as S.E. Hinton rather than Susan on the book; since my subject was gang fights I figured most boys would look at the book and think, 'What can a chick know about stuff like that?'"[3]

STAY GOLD

It turned out that a "chick" could know quite a bit about stuff like that. *The Outsiders* gives an account of several days in the lives of a small group of Tulsa teenagers, a world with no parents and few adults. It begins and ends with the same lines: "When I stepped out into the bright sunlight from the darkness of the movie house, I had only two things on my mind: Paul Newman and a ride home." (Paul Newman was a major American movie star who often played glamorously rebellious characters in movies such as *Hud* and *Cool Hand Luke*.) Indeed, at the end of the novel it becomes clear that the entire book is a composition that the story's narrator, Ponyboy Curtis, is writing for his English class assignment. Ponyboy lives with his older brothers, Sodapop and Darry, (their parents were killed in a car crash eight months before the events of the novel begin) in a tough neighborhood in the "wrong" part of Tulsa.

Followed home from the movies by a group of Socs, Ponyboy is attacked but saved by his brothers, along with other members of his gang, the greasers—Dallas Winston, the tough guy, and Two-Bit Matthews, a joker who also carries a switchblade. Later that night, Ponyboy, Dallas, and another gang member, Johnny, sneak into a drive-in movie and start talking to two girls who are Socs, Cherry and Marcia. They are confronted after the movie by more Socs, led by Cherry's boyfriend, Bob Sheldon, but Cherry stops a potential fight by leaving with the other Socs. Ponyboy and Johnny then hang out in a vacant lot discussing their lives, where we learn that Johnny also lacks a regular family structure: His father abuses him both physically and emotionally. Indeed, the gang is really Johnny's only family. As Ponyboy points out, "If it hadn't been for the gang,

Johnny would never have known what love and affection are."[4] The boys also express their desire to be somewhere else, "someplace without greasers or Socs, with just people. Plain ordinary people."[5]

The boys fall asleep in the lot. When Ponyboy arrives home much later than expected, he gets into a fight with Darry, who has been waiting up for him. After Darry explodes in anger and slaps him, Ponyboy runs out of the house, meets up with Johnny, and the two plan to run away for good. They only get as far as the park when Sheldon and the Socs meet up with them again, ready to get back at the greasers for daring to talk and walk with "their" girls. When it looks like the Socs are going to drown Ponyboy in the fountain, Johnny pulls out a knife and kills Sheldon, ending the fight as the remaining Socs flee.

Now Ponyboy and Johnny *have* to flee town. Dallas gives them directions to a deserted church in a nearby town, where they hide for the next five days. There they spend their time cutting off and dying their hair in an effort to hide their identities, eating bologna sandwiches, watching the sun rise and set, reading the novel *Gone with the Wind*, and discussing the Robert Frost poem "Nothing Gold Can Stay," particularly the poem's two final lines, "So dawn goes down to day/Nothing gold can stay."

This poem and the boys' interest in it illuminates many of the main themes of the book. The mere fact that Ponyboy has memorized the poem demonstrates that there are depths to him that go beyond his outer greaser appearance. For Ponyboy, the poem's meanings are elusive; he tells Johnny that "He [Robert Frost] meant more to it than I'm getting though."[6] The poem seems to him to be about pessimism and loss, but he knows it is about more than just that. By the end of the book, Johnny will reveal to Ponyboy his own interpretation of the poem.

Dallas drives to the church to meet with the boys, and Johnny decides it is time to stop running and turn himself into the police. After eating at a restaurant, the boys pass the church on their way home and see that it is on fire. Learning that a group of children are inside, and worried that the fire was their own fault, Ponyboy and Johnny both rush into the church in an attempt to save the kids. Although the children are rescued, Johnny is badly hurt when a piece of timber falls on his back. Dallas was burned on the arm.

Now thought of as heroes for saving the children, Ponyboy goes to visit Johnny at the hospital, where he is listed in critical condition. Later that evening, there is a major rumble between the Socs and the greasers, which the greasers win. Ponyboy and Dallas hurry to the hospital to share the good news with Johnny, only to discover that he is near death. With his dying words, Johnny tells Ponyboy to "Stay gold," referring, of course, to the Robert Frost poem. Dallas, devastated by Johnny's death, robs a grocery store and runs out into the street, where the police shoot and kill him when he points an unloaded gun at them.

Ponyboy, distraught at the death of his friends, convinces himself that he, not Johnny, killed Bob. He plans to admit to murder at the hearing regarding Bob's death, but the matter is closed before he is able to confess. Ponyboy receives one final message from Johnny: a letter he had written and tucked inside his copy of *Gone with the Wind*. In it, he gives his interpretation of Frost's poem "Nothing Gold Can Stay": "I've been thinking about . . . that poem, that that guy that wrote it, he meant you're gold when you're a kid, like green. When you're a kid everything's new, dawn. It's just like when you get used to everything that it's day. Like the way you dig sunsets, Pony. That's gold. Keep that way, it's a good way to be."[7]

With those words, Ponyboy has a realization about the life he was leading and about all the other kids like him:

> I could picture hundreds and hundreds of boys living on the wrong sides of cities, boys with black eyes who jumped at their own shadows. Hundreds of boys who maybe watched sunsets and looked at stars and ached for something better. I could see boys going down under street lights because they were mean and tough and hated the world, and it was too late to tell them that there was still good in it, and they wouldn't believe you if you did. . . . There should be some help, someone should tell them before it was too late.[8]

That someone is Ponyboy. As the book ends, he sits down at his desk to write the opening sentence of the book just read: "When I stepped out into the bright sunlight from the darkness . . ."[9]

Upon publication, the book received largely glowing reviews. Writing in *Horn Book*, Jane Manthorne called Hinton's work "a remarkable novel . . . a moving credible view of the outsiders from inside."[10] Nat Hentoff, writing for the *Atlantic Monthly*, though mostly criticizing the book's plot, stated that Hinton, "with an astute ear and a lively sense of the restless rhythms of the young, also explores the tenacious loyalties on both sides of the class divide."[11]

Of course, not all reviewers found the book completely worthy of praise. They criticized the plot as being overly melodramatic and sentimental and the writing as cliché. Even those critics found something to praise in the book, however. Thomas Fleming posed the question "Can sincerity overcome clichés?" in the *New York Times Book Review* and went on to answer his own question: "In this book by a now 17-year-old author, it almost does the trick. By almost any standard, Miss Hinton's performance is impressive."[12]

Some reviewers, parents, teachers, and librarians criticized *The Outsiders* for what they saw as its excessive and glamorized violence, which they feared some kids would emulate. Hinton responded to this criticism by noting that some parents who allowed their children to watch violence on television or at the movies for some reason had a different reaction when the violence was on the printed page. She also noted that the violence in *The Outsiders* was anything *but* glamorous and that a price was paid for every violent act.

One parent who had a mixed reaction to *The Outsiders* was Hinton's own mother, who did not read the book until after it had been published. Her first reaction? Shock. According to Hinton, her primary concern was what the neighbors and the rest of the family would think. Then, when *The Outsiders* began to receive good reviews and the money started coming in, her feelings changed to, "Wasn't that a nice little book that Susie wrote?"[13]

At first, the money just trickled in as sales of the book started slowly—Hinton's first royalty check was for just $12—but sales quickly grew due to strong word of mouth and teachers often assigning the book to their English classes, happy to discover a book that their students actually wanted to read. It soon became apparent that Hinton had struck a chord with a vast but previously untapped readership: young kids who wanted to hear their stories told from their perspective with their voices. It didn't matter that most readers of *The Outsiders* did not belong to gangs or have life experiences anything close to those experienced by Ponyboy and his friends. It didn't even matter that Pony-boy's writing style (as the book is supposed to have been written by Ponyboy) is highly literary in a way far beyond what would be expected of him.

What mattered was the fact that kids could identify with Ponyboy and the rest of the characters in *The Outsiders*, who are romantic, and not realistic, representations of young adults. What the characters in *The Outsiders* experience is a heightened sense of what most young adults experience: the need to belong, the fear of not fitting in, the feeling of being an outsider. Readers, whatever their background, are able to relate to the characters, experience what they go through, feel their pain, and understand their friendships. In *The Outsiders*, what truly matters is the characters. Jay Daly said in his book *Presenting S.E. Hinton*, "The book comes to life through its characters and situation, their almost painful yearnings and loyalties, their honesty. While parents and censors argued about violence and sensationalism, the readers responded to the characters, the people."[14]

This is not all surprising. Hinton herself acknowledges that her strength as a writer lies in her characters and not in her plots. In fact, she claims that she can't plot her way to the grocery store! For Hinton, her characters, though fictional, are as real as anyone she knows in real life. By the time she has completed writing a book, she knows everything there is to know about them, as she explained in an interview with Teresa Miller, "I'm a character writer. I know my characters' astrological signs; I know what they eat for breakfast. It doesn't matter whether those details show up in the books themselves. I have to become my narrators the way actors become their characters."[15]

It is through this very process that her novels develop: Character *is* plot. What matters is not so much *what*

*Pictured above, Will Rogers High School as it looked in the 1960s. Forty years after Hinton wrote about gang rivalries in **The Outsiders**, her alma mater still has a significant gang presence. Many of its students who come from impoverished and broken homes identify with the characters in the novel.*

happens, but how the characters *respond* to what happens. Take, for example, the scene in which the church burns down (a scene that Hinton put into the book at the suggestion of her high school friends). The actual event of the church fire is meaningless to the plot—what matters is what the event reveals about the characters.

In another case of how character becomes plot, Hinton was asked in an interview with Teresa Miller if she knew when she started writing *The Outsiders* that Johnny would die or if it was discovered during the process of writing. "I discovered that in process," she said. "To me that's the way the story happened. I didn't make Johnny die; he died."[16]

IMPACT

Today, more than 40 years after its publication, *The Outsiders* is S.E. Hinton's most famous and best loved title, still relevant to teen readers in Tulsa and across the country. Kevin Burr, the principal of Will Rogers High School (Hinton's alma mater and the real-life setting of *The Outsiders*), told CNN: "We have a significant gang presence and a set of issues we have to deal with, but that's part of what resonates with kids about her book."[17] Kim Paper, a ninth-grade English teacher who uses the book in her class, added: "There's a lot of poverty at Will Rogers, a lot of broken families. So kids here can especially identify with Ponyboy and his group. It's what kids that age are thinking about, when they feel kind of isolated from everybody else."[18]

The Outsiders remains Hinton's most controversial book as well: The American Library Association (ALA) listed it as number 41 in the "100 Most Frequently Challenged

Did you know...

Among other projects Hinton has in mind are what she describes as a paranormal/suspense/comedy novel, a screenplay that she would like to make into a movie as well as a novel, and even a historical novel. The paranormal/suspense/comedy novel involves a man who escapes from life in Oklahoma, goes to Los Angeles and makes a lot of money, then returns to Oklahoma to see his family again. While he is in Oklahoma, weird things start to happen, including the appearance of strange lights and the arrival of a black panther.

Books from 1990–2000." According to the American Booksellers Foundation, *The Outsiders* was the third most banned and challenged book between the years of 2004 and 2005.

Though some adults may still argue about the book's content, young readers, for whom the book was written, understand it completely. It is still as relevant, still as vital today as when it was first written. As an older reader posted on Amazon.com, even today, the book hits deeply those who "stay gold":

> I have no idea why this book resonated so deeply with me. I was not raised in Oklahoma. . . . My parents were alive and well and I didn't run with a gang . . . but I identified so much with Ponyboy that it might have been me telling the story. I've read this book at least a dozen times and enjoyed it as much each time as I did the first time. Maybe it's because this book taps into the angst of our teenage years. Even if you aren't in a gang, aren't a greaser or soc, most teenagers go through a period where they feel like they just don't belong. Like they are on the outside looking in. Like they are different from the crowd.[19]

With this one book, S.E. Hinton not only touched generations of readers, she also inspired other writers who were eager to write about the lives of young adults in a new, modern, realistic way. Though excited about her success, Hinton found herself facing an unexpected dilemma. When your first book is as popular and as influential as *The Outsiders*, what do you do for an encore?

S.E. Hinton in 1968. Having become a critically acclaimed and popular author with The Outsiders, *Hinton struggled with writing her second novel,* That Was Then, This Is Now.

4

The Second Novel
Is the Hardest

THE OUTSIDERS CHANGED S.E. Hinton's life. It made her famous in literary circles and with young readers. She was able to leave her hometown of Tulsa for the first time to visit her publisher and do a round of interviews in New York City. Finally, thanks to the growing popularity of her book, she now had money to go to college.

She decided to attend the University of Tulsa and to major in education. Hinton had always been interested in children and hoped that she would be able to translate that interest into a career as a teacher. What she soon learned, however, was that despite her love for children, she was not cut out to teach.

Hinton found her time as a student teacher both physically and emotionally draining. The problem was that she became so emotionally invested in her students that she found herself worrying about them constantly. This also made it difficult to begin work on her second novel.

Hinton had other worries as well. While attending the University of Tulsa, she took a lot of literature courses, which introduced her to many of the world's great novels. Looking back at her own book after reading these classics, she felt that her work was sorely lacking. Indeed, upon rereading *The Outsiders* for the first time at the age of 20, she thought, as quoted in *Presenting S.E. Hinton*, "It was the worst piece of trash I'd ever seen. I magnified its faults: 'Oh no, this thing has my name on it.'"[1]

Depressed by her growing awareness that teaching was not for her, feelings of inadequacy about her book, and a sense of pressure to begin working on a second novel all combined to bring about an author's worst fear: writer's block. What is writer's block? It is usually defined as a temporary loss of the ability to begin or to continue writing. Unfortunately, for some writers it is not always temporary: Some cases of writer's block have gone on for years or even decades. In one famous instance, Henry Roth, whose most famous novel, *Call It Sleep*, was published in 1934, found himself unable to finish another book until 1979—45 years later.

For Hinton, though her period of writer's block was not nearly as long, it was still painful while it lasted. For nearly four years, Susie Hinton, the girl who had been writing for as long as she could remember, found herself unable to even type a letter on the typewriter. Compounding the problem was the pressure placed on her by the success of *The Outsiders*. She had written that book for herself, without a thought of writing for an audience. Now, however, she had an audience waiting breathlessly for her next book. How could she possibly please them? How could her next book be nearly as good as *The Outsiders*? She discussed this problem in an interview with Teresa Miller, "For the first time, I was aware of the audience. When I was writing *The Outsiders*, it was for me; I wasn't thinking about getting published. I still envy those days. I've never written anything with the idea, 'Oh kids will like this,' but in the back of my head now I know that somebody's going to review me."[2]

How did she finally pull out of her writer's block, sit down at her typewriter, and start her new book? Encouragement from her new boyfriend.

His name was David Inhofe; Hinton met him in her freshman biology class. The two began dating and quickly fell in love. Inhofe realized that his girlfriend was depressed about school and her inability to start a new novel, and decided to do what he could to help. To motivate her to start writing again, he used a simple carrot-and-stick approach: If she wrote two pages over the course of the day, he would take her out for the evening. If she didn't, he wouldn't take her out. Because Hinton wanted David to take her out, she wrote the two pages daily. As Hinton said in an autobiographical sketch cited in *Presenting S.E. Hinton*, "David made me write *That Was Then, This Is Now*. When I was writing for fun, I loved it; when it turned into a profession it scared me. I kept thinking, 'You don't know what you're doing.'"[3]

With David's support and encouragement, she kept going, carefully writing her two pages each day, making sure every sentence was perfect before going on to the next.

By 1970, she had piled up what looked to her to be a completed manuscript, and she sent it off to her publisher, hoping for the best. Indeed, 1970 turned out to be a banner year for Hinton. She and David graduated from the University of Tulsa and married three months later, in September. Hinton also received a contract for her new book. She described this to Teresa Miller: "It's funny, because I got the contract on our wedding day. Before, when the contract for *The Outsiders* arrived on graduation day, I thought, 'Graduation is nothing; I sold my book!' But when my contract came for *That Was Then, This Is Now*, I was thinking, 'This is nothing; I'm getting married.'"[4]

THAT WAS THEN, THIS IS NOW

If the brash and over-the-top *The Outsiders* reads like the first novel that it is, her second novel *That Was Then, This Is Now* shows a new maturity in Hinton, a newly found sense of control. If, in some ways, *The Outsiders* feels to the reader as though it somehow wrote itself, *That Was Then, This Is Now* reads like a book written by a writer knowing exactly what she wanted to do. Indeed, anyone who criticized her new book seemed to feel, like Jay Daly, that the book was missing the "spark," the seemingly spontaneous rush of feeling that made *The Outsiders* an immediate classic.

There are obvious similarities between the two books. Both books are set in Tulsa, Oklahoma. Both books feature young heroes who are essentially on their own trying to make sense of their lives while being thrust into situations that test, challenge, and change them. Both books are also told in the first person, a narrative technique that allows the reader to identify and form a bond with the protagonist. As a bonus, the main character from *The Outsiders*, Ponyboy, also makes an appearance in the new book.

That, though, is where the similarities end. *That Was Then, This Is Now* can in no way be considered a sequel to *The Outsiders*. Bryon, who lives with his foster brother, Mark, narrates the book. Mark is described in the book as being "small and compact, with strange golden eyes and hair to match, and a grin like a friendly lion,"[5] and is utterly lacking in morals. Indeed, Hinton said in an interview with William Walsh in *From Writers to Students: The Pleasures and Pains of Writing*, that she "actually got Mark's personality from a cat . . . a completely amoral little animal."[6] It is the changing relationship between Bryon and Mark that is at the heart of the novel.

Mark and Bryon are friends with Charlie, the local bar owner, who allows them to hustle pool in his place to earn a bit of money. They are also friends with M&M, a smart younger kid, who is a loner and hippie. After Mark gets badly beaten in a fight, it is Bryon who looks after him. The boys talk about friendship and old times and how everything is constantly changing, and Mark asks Bryon, "Do you ever get the feeling that the whole world is changing? Like somethin' is coming to an end because somethin' else is beginning,"[7] which leads Bryon to respond with, "That was then, this is now."[8] Bryon falls in love with M&M's sister, Cathy, and this new relationship serves to drive a wedge between him and Mark.

Outside the bar one night, Charlie is shot to death while attempting to rescue Mark and Bryon from two men whom they'd hustled in pool. Around this same time, M&M runs away from home and joins a group of hippies living in an abandoned house. While there, he takes a psychedelic drug and has a "bad trip" from which he may never fully recover. When Bryon learns that Mark has been selling drugs—the same kinds of drugs that M&M took—he calls the police to come and arrest his "brother" and best friend. For the first time, Mark cannot use his personal charm to escape the consequences of his actions. The book ends on a bleak note when, months later, Bryon goes to visit Mark in prison. Mark tells Bryon he hates him. Bryon attempts to get Mark to forgive him, but Mark will have none of it: "'We were like brothers,' I said, desperate. 'You were my best friend—' He laughed again, and his eyes were the golden, hard, flat eyes of a jungle animal. 'Like a friend once said to me, 'That was then, and this is now.'"[9]

The book's last lines, Bryon's final thoughts, offer no comfort to the reader: "And to think, I used to be sure of things. Me, once I had all the answers. I wish I was a kid again, when I had all the answers."[10]

CRITICAL REACTION

That Was Then, This Is Now, with its references to drugs and hippies, is perhaps more dated than the timeless *The Outsiders*, but no less powerful for that. Hinton herself feels that the book is technically a better book than *The Outsiders*, because she had more control over her emotions as she wrote it, and that the book was not as emotionally over-the-top. (Of course, some readers prefer *The Outsiders'* bold emotions to the more coolly written *That Was Then, This Is Now*.) Hinton told Teresa Miller about her newfound control over her writing, "You've got to control emotion with technique. Talent plus discipline equals art; you can't have one without the other."[11]

In many ways, *That Was Then, This Is Now* offers an abandonment of one of the main themes of her earlier book. If "stay gold," was the essence of *The Outsiders*—holding onto one's idealism and innocence—then *That Was Then, This Is Now* urges upon its readers a new lesson: Growing up and shedding one's innocence is a necessary but painful experience. Hinton herself described how the title helps to sum up the book, "I wanted to use it as a metaphor for growing up and suddenly realizing that you can't go on being a little kid. You've got to make some tough decisions. Sometimes they're not going to be the right decisions, but you've got to blunder your way through them."[12]

Was Bryon's emotional decision to turn his "brother" Mark over to the police the right one? Could he have handled it better? Many readers, along with Bryon, have thought and argued about what they would have done in the same situation, and found themselves frustrated and angry

Did you know...

Most people assume that because Hinton seems to understand young adults so well in her books that it must spill over to her real-life relationships. This was not always the case. As often happens in families, when Hinton's son, Nick, became a teenager, his attitude toward his parents changed, and Hinton did not always know how to deal with it. In an interview on CNN.com, she recalled, "It was so strange because the three of us were so compatible, going to restaurants and falling out of our chairs, laughing. When he became a teenager, I was dumbfounded by the hostility. It was like someone shut off the light switch. I was really hurt. You had to walk on tippy-toes." Today, they have a very close and loving relationship again.

over how the book ends. Hinton feels that that is the appropriate response to the book, telling Miller, "I've always said if you threw the book across the room at the end, you understood it. I wanted to show there's not a happy ending for every story. In a lot of ways, growth is betrayal. Things change, no matter how much you'd like them to remain the same."[13]

Indeed, Jay Daly quotes Hinton in his book *Presenting S.E. Hinton* as saying that "No other book has provided the kind of discussion of motives and personal disagreements that *That Was Then, This Is Now* has provoked."[14] Though readers for nearly 40 years have argued over the book, critics have been nearly unanimous in their praise. Michael Cort, writing for the *New York Times*, lauded the book: "The phrase 'if only' is perhaps the most bittersweet in the language, and Miss Hinton uses it skillfully to underline her theme: Growth can be a dangerous process." Despite his reservations about Bryon's self-pity, he concluded that Hinton wrote "a mature, disciplined novel, which excites a response in the reader. Whatever its faults, her book will be hard to forget."[15]

Once read, the book *is* difficult to forget. With her second novel, she had proved that her first book was more than just a fluke: S.E. Hinton was a real writer with something important to say to her readers. The American Library Association agreed, presenting her with its Best Books for Young Adults award in 1971, the year that *That Was Then, This Is Now* was published. It was also chosen as a *Chicago Tribune* "Book World" Spring Book Festival Honor Book that same year.

It was a good period for Hinton. After marrying David Inhofe, the couple traveled across Europe for six months, living like "hippies" in Spain and unwinding from the rigors of Hinton writing her second novel. On returning to the United States, they settled in Palo Alto, California, where David attended graduate school. While David busied himself studying, Hinton began to think about her next novel. It would be a book that would leave book critics sharply divided: Some would call it unsatisfying, and others would call it a true work of art.

A movie still from Rumble Fish, *the second film Francis Ford Coppola adapted from an S.E. Hinton novel. Pictured from left, the actors Laurence Fishburne and Matt Dillon. According to many critics,* Rumble Fish *contains some of Hinton's most complex writing.*

5

It's Called Art

THE BOOK WOULD be called *Rumble Fish*. Its origins were simple: A photograph of a boy and a motorcycle that had been published in the magazine *Saturday Review* in 1967. Fascinated by the photo, Hinton had cut it out of the magazine and carried it around with her for years, certain that someday she would write a story about it. (Curiously enough, many years later, after the publication of *Rumble Fish* and while on a publicity tour for her next novel, *Tex,* Hinton met a high school teacher who approached her with that same photo in hand, not knowing that Hinton had the photograph herself. It turned out that the teacher had also thought that the photo was interesting and had

55

cut it out. He had then made the connection when he read *Rumble Fish*.)

The plot for *Rumble Fish* made its first appearance in a short story of the same name that Hinton wrote for a creative writing class as a student at the University of Tulsa. Looking back on the story years later, she realized that it contained the plot she was looking for, though in a shorter form. As Hinton has said time and time again, plot is the hardest part of the writing process for her. So with the hardest part already in place, she was able to finish the book in only four months.

The one problem she *did* have while writing *Rumble Fish* was determining the proper point of view: Which of the characters would make the best narrator for the story? Steve, a smart, observant, articulate kid, had been her first choice. She realized, though, that her first two books, *The Outsiders* and *That Was Then, This Is Now*, both had narrators (Ponyboy and Bryon) who were equally smart and articulate—and Hinton was interested in writing something from a different perspective.

She rewrote the book from the perspective of Rusty-James, who is *not* smart, who is *not* observant, and who does not necessarily fully understand everything that is going on around him. As Hinton told Teresa Miller, writing from this particular perspective was a challenge: "I'd write a sentence and be proud of it as a writer, look at it again, think Rusty-James could not say that, and cross it out."[1]

RUMBLE FISH

The main story of *Rumble Fish* is set within a framework: The book begins and ends on a beach, several years after the main action of the story has occurred. Rusty-James, the book's narrator, wants nothing more out of life than to be tough, good-looking, and good at everything, just as he sees his older brother, Motorcycle Boy. Motorcycle Boy, described as "a perfect knight"[2] and "the pagan prince,"[3] was the leader of a gang, but now finds himself adrift and looking for meaning in his life. To Rusty-James and their friends, though, he's still a glorious, unknowable hero. Even Hinton found Motorcycle Boy a mystery, telling Teresa Miller: "I haven't got any more clue to what that guy's mind was like than anybody else does. He's an enigma to me."[4]

Hinton did say in an interview:

> Rusty-James sees him one way, which is not right. . . . Motorcycle Boy's flaw is his inability to compromise, and that's why I made him colorblind. He interprets life in "black and white," and he has the ability to walk off and leave everything, which is what ultimately destroys him. . . . Every time I get a letter from a kid who says that *Rumble Fish* is his favorite book, he's usually in the reformatory.[5]

The story within the frame begins with one chillingly simple line, "I was hanging out in Benny's, playing pool, when I heard Biff Wilcox was looking to kill me."[6] Soon enough, Rusty-James is badly cut up in a knife fight, but does not go to the hospital. Instead, his friend Steve and his brother, Motorcycle Boy, take him home and pour wine on the wound to disinfect it. Rusty-James and Motorcycle Boy live in a shabby apartment with their father, a former lawyer, who is usually drunk and absent from their lives.

Despite his wound, Rusty-James goes to school the next day. That night, he goes to an all-night party by the lake. The next day he is expelled from school and loses his girlfriend. To cheer himself up, Rusty-James convinces Motorcycle Boy and Steve to go party with him across the river, at the downtown strip, "where there were lots of people and noise and lights and you could feel energy coming off things, even buildings."[7] Later that night, Rusty-James is hit on the head with a tire iron and almost killed before being saved by Motorcycle Boy. The next night, Motorcycle Boy steals some brightly colored Siamese fighting fish (also known as rumble fish) from a pet store to release into the river and is shot to death by the police.

At story's end, Rusty-James, now color-blind like Motorcycle Boy and alone, is sitting on a beach in California, staring at the waves. Throughout the book, Rusty-James repeatedly expresses his desire to become like his brother, Motorcycle Boy. Now he *has* become his brother, and it's not what he thought it would be. This, of course, was Hinton's point: "Do not identify with something you don't define, because you may be getting it all wrong."[8]

Rumble Fish may be Hinton's shortest and most tightly plotted book for young adults, but it also contains some of her most complex writing. Through her use of symbolism

Did you know...

Several years ago, S.E. Hinton's house was invaded by frogs, and now she collects them! Of course, these frogs are pieces of art which she has everywhere: in her den, in her office, along the bookcases, and even on her desk. The frogs are not placed about in a haphazard manner; instead, they're put together to tell a story. In one case, for example, a frog guards an artificial crow. In another, a frog warily watches the Loch Ness monster.

(the character Motorcycle Boy doesn't have a name), the use of color and color-blindness as metaphors for how people view life, the identification of each character with an animal, the use of the river as a symbol of a divided city and of divided lives, and the role of destiny in the lives of her characters, Hinton creates a dreamlike, almost unreal world.

Some critics felt that Hinton did not manage to successfully pull the book off. Anita Silvey, writing for the *Horn Book Magazine* and quoted in *Presenting S.E. Hinton*, felt that, "By her third book, the outcome for S.E. Hinton seems to be unpromising; her writing has the same style and the same perception as it had when she was sixteen. . . . She is no longer a teenager writing about teenagers today, and the book raises the question, whether as an adult, she will ever have much of importance to say to young readers."[9]

Silvey's opinion, however, was in the minority—most critics raved about Hinton's growth as a writer and as an artist. Margery Fisher, writing for *Growing Point*, remarked: "Of the three striking books by this young author, *Rumble Fish* seems the most carefully structured and the most probing."[10] Jane Abramson in *School Library Journal* concluded that the "stylistically superb *Rumble Fish* packs a punch that will leave readers of any age reeling."[11]

It was Jay Daly, though, in his study of Hinton for *Presenting S.E. Hinton*, who perhaps best summarized Hinton's accomplishment,

In the end we respond to *Rumble Fish* in a much deeper way than we do to *That Was Then, This Is Now*. It's an emotional, almost a physical response, as opposed to the more rational, intellectual reaction that the other book prompted. Whatever its defects . . . *Rumble Fish* works as a novel. In its appeal to the mythic element in life, in its living, breathing creation of the . . . character of Rusty-James, the book works. And there is a name usually given to this kind of success: It is called art.[12]

Rumble Fish went on to win an American Library Association Best Books for Young Adults Award in 1975 and to be named by the *School Library Journal* as one of the Best Books of the Year. It stands today as one of Hinton's finest achievements.

Writing *Rumble Fish* was also one of the most emotionally draining experiences Hinton has had as a writer. She has said on more than one occasion that when she writes, she enters into the mind of the narrator of her novel. So although she enjoyed writing *Rumble Fish*, after finishing it, she was more than happy to move on and become someone other than Rusty-James. As she told Teresa Miller, "By the time I was finished with Rusty-James, I felt like I'd been pounding my head against a wall—a stone wall—and I wanted to be somebody happy for a change."[13]

"I JUST LOVED BEING THAT CHARACTER"

The character's name is Tex McCormick. As mentioned previously, when Hinton writes a book, she thinks about the character and then she actually *becomes* the character. (Interestingly, all of her books for young adults are written from the point of view of a male protagonist. She has explained in several interviews that she spent the first part of her life wanting to be a teenage boy and the second part of her life doomed to being one.)

Hinton admitted that Rusty-James was a difficult character to become. Hinton loved being Ponyboy because he was a lot like her: He had freedom, good friends, and "the things that were important to him were the things that were important to me,"[14] as she said in her article, "On Writing

A movie still from Tex, *a 1982 adaptation of Hinton's novel of the same name, which starred* (from left) *Jim Meltzer and Matt Dillon. Of all the characters Hinton has created, she considers Tex to be her favorite.*

Tex." In that same article, she went on to discuss the character Tex, explaining that although she and Tex were very different, he was the narrator she most enjoyed becoming. "Capable of thinking, he has to be made to think; he relies on instinct instead of intellect. And basically his instincts are good. Capable of violence, but not malice, he has to learn things the hard way—a basically happy person trying to deal with unhappiness. I envied him his total lack of suspicion."[15]

Despite the fact that she truly enjoyed becoming Tex, writing the book proved to be more difficult than she had planned. What was the problem? As has been discussed, Hinton firmly believes that her strength as a writer is in her characters; plot is not, and never has been, her strong point. When writing *Tex*, Hinton would find herself going off on 60-page tangents that had nothing to do with the story she was trying to tell. Often, she would have to put the book away for a period of time, pull it back out, and try again. Finally, after three and a half years of writing, the book was ready to go. It proved to be worth the wait.

TEX

Tex tells the story of Tex McCormick, a 14-year-old boy living with his older brother, Mason. Because their mother had died and their father is often out working on the rodeo circuit, Mason, a high school senior who hopes to go to college on an athletic scholarship, is forced to look after his younger brother, often at the expense of his own hopes and dreams. When the story opens, their father has been away for five months, much longer than usual, and money is tight. Mason is forced to sell off the family horses, including Tex's own horse, Negrito, to pay the bills. Tex's loss of his closest companion adds strain to the already stressed relationship between the two brothers. After a bloody physical confrontation between Tex and Mason, Tex runs away to find his beloved horse. Both his friend Johnny and his sister, Jamie, attempt to talk Tex out of it, to no avail. Mason eventually brings Tex home in their pickup truck.

Tex and Johnny get into trouble on a regular basis, much to the dismay of Johnny's father, Cole Collins, who thinks that Tex is a bad influence on his son. Things become even rougher for Tex and Mason when a hitchhiker—the character Mark from *That Was Then, This Is Now*, who has busted out of jail—kidnaps them. Tex's quick thinking saves him and Mason, but it also gets Mark killed by the police. The resulting news coverage of the event brings the brothers' father home, but the results are disappointing for Tex: His father fails to buy back Negrito, and it is revealed that he is not Tex's biological father.

Further trouble ensues when Tex becomes involved with one of Mason's friends who deals drugs, resulting in Tex ending up in the hospital with a bullet wound. Once recovered, he reconciles with Mason and convinces him to follow his dream of going to college. Tex lines up a job working with horses and realizes that he can take care of himself.

The plot, though perhaps overcomplicated and dramatic, serves its purposes well. The reader is aware of Tex's evolution throughout the story. Of all Hinton's male protagonists, Tex is the one who grows up the most in the course of the book. As Hinton describes him, he's the least tough, but actually the strongest, of her characters. Tex is the one character that the reader can say with confidence is going to survive in the world.

Tex explores many of the same topics that Hinton has examined in her previous works: the idea of being parentless and trying to belong, the fear of being alone, the role of fate and how to survive, evil and hatred, and the differences between those who escape the world in which they're born and those who stay behind. Unlike *That Was Then, This Is Now*, which seemed to many too cool and controlled and too dispassionate to fully resolve the issues presented in it, *Tex*, a warmer, more compassionate work, comes closer to achieving some sort of resolution. At the very least, the reader comes away from reading *Tex* with a sense of hope and optimism.

One interesting aspect of *Tex* is Hinton's use of characters from *That Was Then, This Is Now* (aside from Mark, the hitchhiker, Tex's teacher, Ms. Carlson, is Cathy from that same book). Indeed, *Tex* can be seen as a kind of counterpoint to *That Was Then, This Is Now,* with Hinton trying to make clearer some issues that were felt to be too vague in the earlier book. Like Bryon, Tex learns something bad about somebody in his family. Unlike Bryon, he does not let it destroy his relationships. Hinton told Teresa Miller, "I didn't realize it at the time, but I was writing a different version of *That Was Then, This Is Now,* showing another road not taken."[16]

Ultimately, it is the return of "Mark the Lion" that links the two books and also reveals the links between Mark and Tex. The two are very much alike—they share the same hair and coloring—and, for Tex, the similarities are alarming: "He reminded me of somebody, but I couldn't think who."[17] When Tex and Mason pick up Mark on the side of the road, he has escaped from prison and returned to Tulsa, where he "had business to take care of." That business, it is implied, is his long awaited vengeance on Bryon for turning him in to the police, which turned out to be a disappointing accomplishment for him:

> Waited for it for years, the big revenge trip, and when it came right down to it, it was nothing . . . him lying there looking up at me, and he says "Get it over with," and it was like all the air out of a balloon. All these years of planning, waiting to dig the look on his face, and then I just didn't feel like finishing it. . . . I was just too plain bored. And to think I could have been planning something constructive all this time, like the quickest way out of the country. . . .[18]

By the end of the chapter, with Mark lying dead on the side of the road, Tex realizes who it is that Mark reminds him of—himself. Hinton reveals that Tex and Mark are half-brothers who share the same father—a rodeo rider with golden hair and gold eyes. Unlike Mark, who could not survive his family situation, Tex, despite his difficulties, makes it through basically unscathed: still hopeful, still innocent, still trusting in his relationship with his brother and friends.

Relationships are what the book is about, as Hinton said in the publicity materials for *Tex*, ". . . the best I can come up with is: relationships, which are complicated even for simple people; and maybe love, which can't cure anything but sometimes makes the unbearable bearable; and being a teen-ager, which is problem enough for anybody. Mainly it's about Tex McCormick. . . . I have to admit he's a favorite child."[19]

Why is Tex considered to be Hinton's best-loved character? One factor is what Jay Daly calls Tex's "generosity of spirit."[20] When driving down the highway, for example, he doesn't just see cars and strangers. Illustrating this, he asks Mason, "Did you ever think that all those people in those cars have a whole separate story to them, that it's just as important to them as our stuff is to us, and we don't know anything about it." His generosity of spirit even extends to Mark the Lion, telling Mason after the kidnapping was over, "Something really bad must have happened to that guy,"[21] for him to do such a thing. Tex's spirit—generous, forgiving, and always hopeful—is what makes reading *Tex* such a memorable experience.

Hinton's "favorite child" was the favorite of many critics as well. Marilyn Kaye wrote in *School Library Journal*,

"Personal discoveries emerge from the action in a natural, unpretentious . . . way as Hinton explores questions about responsibility, friendship, desire, and communication."[22] Margery Fisher, a longtime Hinton admirer, noted in *Growing Point* that "in this new book Susan Hinton has achieved that illusion of reality which any fiction writer aspires to and which few ever completely achieve."[23]

In contrast, some critics pointed out flaws of the book. Paxton Davis, writing for the *New York Times*, remarked: "There's too much going on here. Even by the standards of today's fiction, S.E. Hinton's vision of contemporary teen-age life is riper than warrants belief. . . . [*Tex* is] busier and more melodramatic than the real life it purports to show."[24] Lance Salway, commenting in *Signal*, agreed that the book was highly theatrical but added that "a writer as good as Hinton can carry it off effortlessly; one believes implicitly in the characters and cares what happens to them."[25]

In his book *Shakespeare: The Invention of the Human*, Harold Bloom confessed that he reads constantly because he cannot, on his own, get to know enough people in a profound enough way to satisfy himself. One of the main reasons we read, he suggests, is to get to know characters that we might not otherwise get to meet in real life. This is what makes *Tex*, as well as Hinton's other young adult novels, so special: In them she creates characters in whom the reader believes and about whom they care deeply.

Tex continued Hinton's streak of popular, award-winning novels. In 1979, the book received the Best Books for Young Adults Award given by the American Library Association and was named a *School Library Journal* Best Book of the Year. Unfortunately for her readers, *Tex* was also the last book she would write for the next decade. Ironically, those years would see her books reach new heights of popularity, as her professional and personal lives moved in new, exciting, and surprising directions.

Pictured above, S.E. Hinton and Matt Dillon in 1982. Unlike many authors who have little if nothing to do with film adaptations of their work, Hinton was deeply involved with the adaptations of her novels and became very close to the actors, including Dillon.

6

From the Page to the Screen

THE PERIOD FROM 1982 to 1985 was an extraordinary time in S.E. Hinton's professional life. All four of her books written to that date, *The Outsiders*; *That Was Then, This Is Now*; *Rumble Fish*; and *Tex*, were made into feature-length films that were popular and critical successes. Whereas most authors of books that are made into films have little to do with the process, Hinton was deeply involved in the filmmaking of her novels.

Hinton had always been a big fan of movies. The first movie she ever saw was the Walt Disney animated film *Peter Pan*, when she was just five years old. (In interviews, she has admitted that watching it helped her to develop crushes on redheaded boys all through grade school.) Of course, as an animal lover, she watched and cried over *Old Yeller* more times than she could count.

As Hinton grew up, her tastes in movies evolved. She embraced more adult films, such as the screen epic *Lawrence of Arabia* and the musical *Bye Bye Birdie*. Though she had always considered herself to be a movie buff, she wasn't at all sure that she wanted *her* books to be turned into films. She saw them as books, not as films, and, like most other writers, she had doubts that they could be translated from the page to the screen in a way that was true to her vision. She would soon be convinced that she was wrong—films that she would be happy with could be made from her books.

TEX

The first of Hinton's novels to be filmed was, ironically, the last of her four books to be published: *Tex*. In 1979, Tim Hunter, a writer at the time who went on to direct *Tex*, had written a screenplay for a movie called *Over the Edge*. While filming was underway, Hunter asked the young actors on the set what books they liked, and they all said books by S.E. Hinton. Matt Dillon, who was making his debut in the film, even told Hunter that if they should ever make a film of a Hinton novel, he wanted to be in it. (Dillon would go on to appear in three of the four films made from Hinton's novels.)

Several years later, representatives from the Walt Disney Company approached Hinton about purchasing the film rights for *Tex*. Initially, she had her doubts, as she said in an interview with the *New York Times* in 1983, "At first I said, 'No, thank you. I'm not interested in doing a Disney movie.' I thought they'd really sugar it up, take out all the sex, drugs and violence and leave nothing but a story of a boy and his horse."[1]

It took a personal visit to Tulsa by Disney vice president Tom Wilhite to convince her that Disney was committed to making a film that was true to her book. Hinton agreed, but with one stipulation: Her horse, Toyota, would have to play the part of Tex's horse, Negrito, in the film. With that agreed upon, the deal was made.

The movie was shot on location in Tulsa. Director Tim Hunter approached Hinton to help scout locations—places in Tulsa that would look right for the various scenes in the movie. Hinton was involved in other ways as well: She helped select actors and rewrote bits of dialogue while the film was being shot. She also made her film debut in *Tex*, playing the small "cameo" role of the typing teacher. Though nervous at first, she soon got the hang of acting, nailing her lines in just two takes.

Hinton even gave Matt Dillon riding lessons for two weeks before filming started so that he and Toyota would be comfortable with each other. Her secret for this? She told Dillon to always keep carrots in his pocket. If you watch the movie carefully, there is one scene where you can spot Toyota nuzzling Dillon's pockets looking for carrots. (Interestingly, Dillon was surprised the first time he met Hinton. He's quoted by Hinton in an interview with Teresa Miller as saying, "Hey, S.E., I thought you was a man!"[2])

Hinton was pleased with the way the film turned out and is still convinced that Dillon's performance in the film is one of his best. The film holds a special place in her heart for another reason as well: Since her horse, Toyota, is now deceased, she only has to watch the movie to see him again, in his prime.

S.E. Hinton on the set with film director Francis Ford Coppola. Initially uninterested in having her books made into movies, Hinton was eventually persuaded by Coppola, best known for The Godfather, The Godfather: Part II, *and* Apocalypse Now.

MEETING FRANCIS FORD COPPOLA

At the same time that Disney was approaching Hinton about the possibility of filming *Tex*, another film director was trying to convince her to let him make a film of her most popular and beloved book, *The Outsiders*. His name was Francis Ford Coppola.

At the time, Coppola was close to the peak of his career as one of America's greatest film directors. The list of his films, which includes *The Godfather*; *The Godfather, Part II*; *The Conversation*; and *Apocalypse Now*, reads like an honor roll of some of the greatest films of the 1970s. Coppola was known for being a director who made tough, adult films, so why would he be interested in making a movie aimed at younger audiences?

It turned out that, similar to *Tex*, Coppola's interest was brought about by an appeal from Hinton's fans. As Hinton told the *New York Times*, "I thought it was really neat that in both those cases, it was my readers who had got the film-makers interested."[3] Coppola had received a letter from a group of kids in California telling him that *The Outsiders* was their favorite book and pleading with him to make it into a movie. Intrigued, he read the book, loved it, and asked his producers to contact Hinton about buying the movie rights.

Following the book's publication, people interested in filming *The Outsiders* approached Hinton time and time again. She had always turned them down, fearing, as she told Teresa Miller, "it was going to end up being *Ponyboy Meets Beach Blanket Bingo*."[4] Francis Ford Coppola was a different story. In addition to his obvious talent as a film-maker, Hinton had recently seen a movie that his company had produced—the film version of the children's classic *The Black Stallion*. Watching it, she was convinced Walter

Farley, the author of the book *The Black Stallion*, would have been happy with how the film turned out. Coppola would be the director to bring *The Outsiders* to the big screen.

WORKING WITH FRANCIS

As with the filming of *Tex*, Hinton was intimately involved in the making of *The Outsiders*. Shooting took place on location in Tulsa, and Hinton assisted Coppola with scouting for locations, selecting wardrobe, and writing the screenplay. The two quickly became good friends. Coppola was lavish in his praise of Hinton, telling the *New York Times*, "When I met Susie, it was confirmed to me that she was not just a young people's novelist, but a real American novelist. For me the primary thing about her books is that the characters come across as very real. Her dialogue is memorable, and her prose is striking. Often a paragraph of her descriptive prose sums up something essential and stays with you."[5]

Initially, Hinton was nervous about meeting Coppola, but the two soon settled into an easy working relationship while writing the screenplay for *The Outsiders*. Coppola would take a copy of the book and color code it, outlining introspective scenes in one color, action in one color, and dialogue in another. He would then cut it up, paste it together in the form of a screenplay, and hand it off to Hinton, asking her to rewrite it for him.

Although Hinton had never written a full screenplay (only a small amount of dialogue for *Tex*), she had learned one valuable lesson from Tim Hunter: He told her that one can never have actors say more than three lines at time or "it sounds like they're giving the preamble of the Constitution."[6] So, in the interest of keeping things moving, Hinton had no problem in cutting lines. Problems arose instead when she tried to change the book's original lines to lines that she now thought sounded better. Coppola would have none of these changes. They were making the movie for the book's readers, who would be upset if new lines were said in place of the lines they remembered from the book.

Working on a movie set was a new experience for Hinton. Growing up, and then later as a writer, she had always been a loner. Making movies, however, is a collaborative effort. "It's the first time I've ever felt at home in a group situation," she told the *New York Times*. "I've never been a joiner. In Tulsa I have a reputation for being slightly eccentric. Even my close friends think I'm a little nutty. But with the movie people I was accepted instantly." And as an added bonus, "There's one other nice thing about the movies. There's always somebody else to blame. With a novel, you have to take all the blame yourself."[7]

Did you know...

S.E. Hinton is not the youngest person to write and publish a novel. One of the very youngest published novelists was English writer Margaret Mary Julia Ashford, better known by her pen name, Daisy Ashford. Born in 1881, Ashford is most famous for her first book, *The Young Visiters, or, Mister Salteena's Plan*, which she wrote when she was just nine years old! This novella, which pokes fun at the upper class society of late nineteenth-century England, was published in 1919, preserving her youthful spelling and punctuation, including "Visiters" in the title. Still in print, the BBC made it into a TV movie in 2003.

Hinton in August 1982, during her involvement with the filming of her novels. Hinton worked closely with Coppola, with whom she wrote the screenplays.

Filming for *The Outsiders* went smoothly. The cast, who were virtual unknowns at the time, including such now-famous actors as C. Thomas Howell as Ponyboy, Rob Lowe as Sodapop, Patrick Swayze as Darry, Matt Dillon as Dallas, Tom Cruise as Steve, Ralph Macchio as Johnny, and Diane Lane as Cherry. Hinton found herself playing "mother" to most of the young cast, who were left largely on their own in Tulsa with no adult supervision. She would advise them, help them, even run lines with them. "The boys depended on me a lot," Hinton told the *New York Times*. "I was kind of a greaser den mother, and they were always consulting me."[8] Rob Lowe even took to calling Hinton "mom" during the course of the filming!

Hinton herself agreed with Lowe's assessment of her, telling CNN that, "I was a mother to all of them, and I wouldn't take any guff from any of them. If one of them acted up, I'd crack the whip and say, 'I'm going to cut your lines.' They were these goofy teenage boys, no adult guidance, no nothing. They wore me out."[9]

Even still, filming went so well that halfway through shooting *The Outsiders*, Coppola turned to Hinton and said, "Susie, we get along great. Have you written anything else I can film?"[10] Hinton told him about *Rumble Fish*, he read it, loved it, and wanted to start production immediately.

"I know what we can do," he told Hinton. "On our Sundays off, let's write a screenplay, and then as soon as we wrap *The Outsiders*, we'll take a two-week break and start filming *Rumble Fish*." Hinton replied, "Sure, Francis, we're working 16 hours a day, and you want to spend Sundays writing another screenplay?"[11] But that's exactly what they did.

By that stage, nothing Coppola did on the set could surprise her. "Working for Francis," she recalled, "I could never tell when he was going to turn to me and say, 'Susie, we'll need a new scene here to make this play.' I could have it for him in three minutes, and it was pretty good, too."[12]

The pair completed the first draft of the screenplay for the new film in just two weeks, and filming for *Rumble Fish*, starring Matt Dillon as Rusty-James, Mickey Rourke as Motorcycle Boy, and Diane Lane as Patty, began on schedule just two weeks after shooting for *The Outsiders* wrapped. This time around, Hinton took a more hands-off approach. Most of the filming was done at night, it was a more difficult shoot, and, except for filming a brief cameo appearance (as she also did in *The Outsiders*), she had little to do with the day-to-day filming.

Both films were released in 1983, each with their own individual style and look. *The Outsiders* is very colorful and lush looking, with a classic over-the-top style that precisely mirrors the emotional range of the book. *Rumble Fish*, on the other hand, is much more stylized, shot in a dramatic black and white (with the exception of the Siamese fighting fish, which were shot in color), to reflect the colorblind way in which Motorcycle Boy sees the world. Hinton was pleased with both films, praising *Rumble Fish* in particular to Teresa Miller, telling her that ". . . [Coppola] was one of the few people I've ever talked to who understood the book. It was about myth-making. The movie's much more visual, much stronger than the book, actually. It was an amazing experience for me as a writer to see Francis's interpretation, because it was just what I was thinking."[13]

One issue that Hinton had with the film of *The Outsiders* was with the changes that were made after filming had ended. Coppola had shot a relatively lengthy screenplay that incorporated the entire book but, under pressure from the studio who felt that the movie was too long, he was forced to cut anything that didn't keep the plot moving in a straight line. Hinton didn't feel she was in a position to complain, but fans of the book did protest, writing Coppola letters asking why their favorite parts of the book had been left out. In September 2005, Coppola released a new version of the film containing 22 minutes of additional footage and new music, entitled *The Outsiders: The Complete*

Version, putting back previously deleted scenes that brought this version closer to the original novel. At last, Coppola and Hinton's film vision was available to fans of both the book and the original film.

THAT WAS THEN, THIS IS NOW

As of 2008, the last of Hinton's books to be made into a movie was *That Was Then, This Is Now*, released in 1985. Unlike the previous three films, Hinton had nothing to do with the filming process. Emilio Estevez, a young actor who had appeared in *Tex* and *The Outsiders*, had obtained the film rights to *That Was Then, This Is Now* and made the decision to both write the screenplay and star in the film as Mark Jennings.

Many people questioned the wisdom of allowing a 20-year-old actor to write a movie screenplay, but Hinton immediately pointed out that she was the same age as Estevez when she wrote the original book. Unfortunately for fans of the book, the studio forced Estevez to make changes in the movie—making it obvious that Mark personally sells the drugs to M&M rather than leaving it more ambiguous, and making the ending nostalgic rather than bitter. These changes watered down the movie, making it, according to Hinton, "wishy-washy."[14]

Hinton had enjoyed her time as part of the film-making process, and her time working with young actors had helped to energize her in ways she had not anticipated. She decided, however, that it was time to get back to her "real" life as a writer and wife. "I still think of myself as a novelist," she told the *New York Times*. ". . . and with the next book I'm doing everything I can to make it unfilmable."[15] Her new novel would be her most complex, demanding, and thoughtful work to date.

S.E. Hinton, in October 1998, on the evening she was inducted into the Oklahoma Writers Hall of Fame at the Philbrook Museum of Art in Tulsa.

7

Back to Work

I don't think I have a masterpiece in me, but I do know I'm writing well in the area I choose to write in. I understand kids and I really like them. And I have a very good memory. I remember exactly what it was like to be a teenager that nobody listened to or paid attention to or wanted around. I mean, it wasn't like that with my family, but I knew a lot of kids like that and hung around with them. They were street kids, gang kids, sort of scrounging around, and somehow I always understood them. They were my type.[1]

—S.E. Hinton

THERE WAS A gap of nine years between the publication of *Tex* and Hinton's next book, *Taming the Star Runner*. There were movies to be made, and then, while settling back to work as a novelist, she discovered that she and her husband were going to have a baby. Hinton immediately wrote to her editors, telling them that she wouldn't be able to begin work on the book right away and politely asked if they wanted their money back. They told her not to worry, to keep the money and start working again whenever she was ready. She didn't look at the book again until her son, Nick, was four years old. At that point, she put him into preschool three days a week and was able to start working again on her next novel.

On the surface, the finished book seems much like Hinton's previous work. The observant reader, though, will notice a difference in the book's first line: "His boot felt empty without his knife in it."[2] For the first time, Hinton had abandoned her usual first-person narrative for a third-person narrative—it's not "My boot . . . ," it's "His boot . . . ." Why the change? As Hinton told Teresa Miller, the change in voice was due to her son: "When I'm writing a first-person narration, I really have to become my own narrator, and I have to be totally involved with that narrator. My son was only four years old at the time, and I was emotionally involved with him. I didn't have anything to spare to become Travis at that point."[3]

Despite the difference of the book being written in the third person, it's still told from the point of view of a young male. Some critics have pointed out that one of Hinton's weaknesses as a novelist is an inability to create female characters who are as strong and as interesting as her male characters. She argues, though, that she writes about what she knows and understands, and, by writing from a male perspective, she is able to reach both male and female readers. It is understood that, typically, girls will read books that are written for boys, but boys won't read books that are written for girls. In the character of Casey the horse trainer, Hinton creates a female character that is as strong and interesting as the male lead. (Of course, in another interview, Hinton said that "writing from a male point of view always came easily for me; being a lazy person, I will usually take the easiest way."[4])

Taming the Star Runner tells the story of 15-year-old Travis Harris, an aspiring writer, who is sent to live with his uncle on his Oklahoma ranch instead of to juvenile hall. Why juvenile hall? The story reveals that he nearly killed his stepfather with a fireplace poker after Travis caught him burning the stories he had written.

What follows is a classic story of city boy goes to the country. Travis arrives in the middle of his uncle's divorce and finds him distant and distracted. Feeling isolated and alone, unable to make friends with those he sees as the hicks and jocks in his new school, and constantly getting into trouble, he begins hanging out in a barn on his uncle's property—a barn that is rented to Casey Kincaid. Casey, three years older than Travis and a horse trainer, is trying to train a nearly untamable horse named Star Runner. The horse is all energy and potential.

The growing relationship between Travis and Casey is at the heart of the book, but there is one other major element of the story: A New York publisher has accepted the manuscript for Travis' book. Of course, there is a hitch. Travis is not yet of legal age, so his mother would have to sign the contract for him. She is reluctant to do so because Travis' stepfather is concerned that he does not come across well in the book. Eventually, Travis' mother stands up to his stepfather and gives permission for Travis to have his book published.

In typical Hinton fashion, the publication of Travis's book is the only happy ending the book offers the reader. Star Runner is killed in an electrical storm, his pure untamed energy unable to survive in the real world. Travis's uncle is forced to sell the ranch, and Casey must find a new home for her horses and lessons. Despite this, Travis has matured and become more "tamed," he has grown close to his uncle, remains good friends with Casey, and is beginning to have romantic feelings for a girl named Jennifer. He has also begun to figure out who he is. At the beginning of the book, Travis continually looks in the mirror to examine himself, but by the book's end, he gazes out the window, watching other people. Perhaps most importantly, as the book ends, Travis has begun work on his next book: "He pulled his chair up to the desk and rolled a blank piece of paper into his typewriter. He sat there, waiting."[5]

Obviously, *Taming the Star Runner* contains direct autobiographical elements new to Hinton's work. Much of Hinton's experiences while writing *The Outsiders*, as well as her early publishing experiences, are given over to Travis in the book. Like Hinton, "Travis couldn't remember when he'd first known he was going to be a writer."[6] Like Hinton, he sends his unsolicited manuscript to a New York publisher, where it is miraculously chosen for publication. Like Hinton, Travis has problems spelling. Like Hinton, Travis gets a "D" in his creative writing class. Like Hinton, Travis is dragged away from his room and typewriter to watch television with the family. Like Hinton, Travis is weak in drawing realistic female characters, and, in a meeting in Tulsa, Travis tells his editor, "I'll clean up the language some, but I ain't going to turn it into a romance. Let the guys read it—there's nothing for guys to read anyway, if you're not into sci-fi. . . . I don't know what girls do, so

I don't write about them. And that junk they like to read makes me barf."[7]

Also, like Hinton, Travis's publisher points out the strengths and weaknesses of his manuscript, and what he'll have to do to make his next book better: "[There is] more style than you know what to do with. It's so full of energy, so sincere, you'll be able to get away with the melodramatics. But not twice, Travis. The critics won't be indulgent twice. You'll have to use some discipline on the next one."[8] Which, of course, is exactly what Hinton did when writing *That Was Then, This Is Now*.

Indeed, as Jay Daly points out in *Presenting S.E. Hinton*, in many ways, *Taming the Star Runner* is the book that *That Was Then, This Is Now* tried to be. It contains many of the same themes: time and the difficulty of change, the concept of free will against that of fate and destiny, the need for individual discipline and growth, and the results of a loss of innocence. Whereas for many readers the themes and motivations in *That Was Then, This Is Now* remained murky and unsatisfying, by the time Hinton wrote *Taming the Star Runner*, she had achieved enough artistic distance

---

Did you know...

In addition to the film version, *The Outsiders* was also turned into a television series. It ran for 14 weeks on the Fox Network in 1990 before being cancelled. Among the cast were Billy Bob Thornton and David Arquette, in his very first acting role as Keith "Two-Bit" Matthews.

S.E. Hinton answering questions during an interview in Tulsa in September 2007. Although best known as being the author of **The Outsiders,** *Hinton continues to publish popular novels. Overall, critics have enjoyed the evolution of her writing throughout her career.*

to be able to clearly write the book she had wanted to write 17 years earlier.

For S.E. Hinton herself, the book *is* about the need for an artist to learn discipline. Travis, watching Casey train her horses, is able to see how discipline transforms a horse into a work of art. Hinton told Miller that "By the end of the book, Travis realizes what [he and Casey] have in common—he's sitting at his typewriter waiting for his next book, and she's waiting for the artistic challenge of her next horse."[9]

CRITICAL RESPONSE

Critics, by and large, appreciated the ever-growing maturity and complexity of Hinton's work. Nancy Vasilakis wrote in *Horn Book* that it "has generally been agreed that no one can speak to the adolescent psyche in the way S.E. Hinton can,"[10] and that with her fifth novel she "hasn't lost her touch."[11] Writing in the *New York Times Book Review*, Patty Campbell noted, "Hinton has produced another story of a tough young Galahad in black T-shirt and leather jacket. The pattern is familiar, but her genius lies in that she has been able to give each of the five protagonists she has drawn from this mythic model a unique voice and a unique story."[12] Later in the review, she noted: "S.E. Hinton continues to grow in strength as a young adult novelist."[13]

Jay Daly was perhaps her most perceptive critic:

> *Taming the Star Runner* emerges as Hinton's most mature and accomplished work. The book is carefully crafted, with much discipline, but the discipline and craft rarely show, so that the story seems to proceed effortlessly on a number of levels. . . . [The book] makes more demands of its readers than the earlier books did. Because so much of the action of the novel is inner action, psychological development, the book requires a more attentive reader. But the rewards are greater, also.[14]

Taming the Star Runner went on to win the American Library Association Best Books for Young Adults award. It would also be the last book S.E. Hinton would write for seven years. Instead, she concentrated her energy and emotions on being a mother for Nick. As she indicated in interviews, with all of her focus on her family, there was nothing left for the page.

*S.E. Hinton, photographed at a hotel in Tulsa in September 2004, the year
she published her first novel for adults,* **Hawkes Harbor.**

8

Branching Out

SOMETIMES IT IS difficult to imagine writers being anything other than writers. It's hard for their fans to picture them having ordinary, everyday lives away from the computer keyboard. S.E. Hinton, like every other writer, does have a life away from the computer. She is a wife and mother. She also has other interests outside of writing. For the seven-year period between writing *Taming the Star Runner* and her next project, she fully embraced all of these aspects of "normal life."

Indeed, Hinton's life is astonishingly normal. She loves to read everything from biographies to history, to social commentary to books about the paranormal, and, of course, fiction, including elaborately plotted Victorian era novels, Mary Renault, and F. Scott Fitzgerald. The works of Jane Austen are a special favorite. Hinton makes sure to read each of Austen's six completed novels (which include *Pride and Prejudice* and *Emma*) once a year. What does Hinton learn from Austen? She marvels at Austen's ability to reveal character through the use of dialogue, an aspect of writing that stands out as one of Hinton's greatest gifts as well. Hinton also takes classes at a local university in order to continue to broaden her education.

Of course, as anyone who has read any of her books would guess, Hinton has long been an avid horsewoman. She bought her beloved horse, Toyota, when she was just 20 years old with the last $75 she had in the bank. She raised him from a colt, and then trained with him to become a champion jumper. When he died at the age of 23, she was there with him as well, making certain that the last thing he heard was her voice. Today she owns a small trail horse.

As Hinton herself told one interviewer, people would generally be amazed at how ordinary her everyday life is: "People think I have been sitting here in an ivory tower with minions or something. But I've been wandering around the Safeway wondering what to cook for dinner like everybody else."[1]

For Hinton, her writing self is kept separate from her other selves. She feels that writing is just one aspect of who she is. She's equally proud of being a good horsewoman, a mother, a friend, and a good cook. By keeping her success as a writer in perspective, it has allowed her to remain remarkably balanced, despite the extraordinary success she has achieved as a writer.

Although "real life" had definite appeal, at heart, Hinton remained a writer. As she said in an interview with bookreporter.com, "It's all I ever wanted to do—I began in grade school—and it's all I know how to do."[2] It was only a matter of time before she returned to the typewriter, but the next books she wrote were different from anything she'd written before.

A NEW AUDIENCE

In 1995 Hinton published two picture books written for elementary-school age children. The first of these books, *Big David, Little David*, is one of her most autobiographical. The story is based on a joke that Hinton and her husband played on their son, Nick, when he was in kindergarten. In the book (and in real life), Nick came home from school and told his parents that there was a boy in class who looked just like his father, with the same hair and glasses—he even had the same name. Confused, Nick asked his father "He's not you, is he?" Nick's parents (both in the book and in real-life), decided to pull a joke on him, and convinced him that that little David and big David were the same person, that every day big David shrunk himself down so that he could go to school with his son. Finally, though, at parents' night at school, Nick sees both his father and little David in the same place at the same time and realizes that they are in fact *not* the same person.

Despite the fact that the book had much less text than Hinton's previous books, writing it proved to be quite a challenge for her. Not only did she have to cut down on her usual grit and realism, she also had to learn to write using considerably fewer words. Eventually, with her editor's help and encouragement, Hinton was able to reduce the word count to the right level for the book's target audience. Unfortunately, many critics felt that Hinton's talents were not an ideal match for a book for such young readers, and most considered the book's concept to be over the head of its intended audience. Hinton herself agreed that writing the book was not as satisfying as writing for her usual young adult audience, telling Teresa Miller that "it was right for that time in my life, because I wasn't ready to get totally involved in writing another novel. I wanted to be creative, but I just didn't have the energy or even the interest to delve into a novel, which takes a whole lot of focus, and, for me, a lot of emotional energy."[3]

In her next book, *The Puppy Sister*, Hinton tells the story of Aleasha, a puppy who doesn't want to remain a puppy, but wants to become a person like her owner, Nick. Gradually, over the course of the book, Aleasha turns human—shedding her fur, learning to stand on legs, starting to speak—becoming the little sister that Nick had longed for.

Critics by and large responded warmly to *The Puppy Sister*. The reviewer for *Publishers Weekly* proclaimed: "With this whimsical animal story, Hinton serves up an entry as memorable in its genre as her classic *The Outsiders* is

Did you know...

S.E. Hinton no longer makes personal appearances. She doesn't like to travel, she doesn't like speaking in public, and, after 30 years of making appearances, she's had enough of it. There's another reason as well: She has come to realize that it is the book that matters, not the writer. She would rather just have her writing speak for itself.

in YA literature. . . . Offering a unique consistently witty account of growing pains and family life, this irresistible fantasy can take its place alongside *Stuart Little* and *Babe the Gallant Pig*."[4]

PART ADVENTURE, PART HORROR

I felt trapped writing teenage books with drama and meaning— or no meaning—and I wanted to go back to when writing was really fun.[5]

—S.E. Hinton

Nick was growing up, and Hinton was ready to once again become a full-time writer. Following *The Puppy Sister*, Hinton switched gears once again. She was also eager to try something new. Why an adult novel at this time? As she told bookreporter.com, "I was living with a teenager and it's hard to work up much sympathy for them in those conditions. Also, I just plain wanted to write about adult characters for a change."[6]

Inspired by re-reading Robert Louis Stevenson's classic novel of pirates and swashbuckling, *Treasure Island*, and Charles Dickens's autobiographical novel, *David Copperfield*, it took Hinton five years to research and write *Hawkes Harbor*. Part adventure, part horror, it was a completely new direction for Hinton as a writer.

Hawkes Harbor tells the story of Jamie Summers, an orphan raised unhappily by nuns who escapes to a life at sea. Living a life filled with thrilling adventures, including pirate battles, gun running, and shark attacks, Summers finally meets his match in the personage of Grenville Hawkes, a vampire to whom he becomes bound as a servant for eternity.

Although the book moves back and forth in time and geography, from the 1950s to the present and from Burma to the United States, the relationship between Summers and Hawkes is the very heart of the story. The story itself is revealed in a series of flashbacks and flash-forwards, as Jamie gradually reveals his story to his psychiatrist, Dr. McDevitt, at the Terrace View Asylum.

The book's protagonist is in some ways similar to Hinton's other boy heroes—he is also a street-tough orphan trying to cope in a hostile world. Of course, none of Hinton's other protagonists had to contend with pirates and vampires. In addition, none of Hinton's other main characters get involved in the kinds of sexual situations that Summers does, but that was one of the reasons that Hinton wrote the book—to test whether or not she was capable of pulling off such scenes.

Critics were mixed in their response to *Hawkes Harbor*, with many expressing the view that the book's mixture of adventure, comedy, and supernatural elements did not quite come together to make a successful book. Calling the book "a shambles," Elizabeth Hand wrote in the *Washington Post*: "It's sad, and depressing, to read a bad book by a writer one respects."[7] Despite the critical drubbing, Hinton herself remained proud of her attempt, and felt that the characters in the book were among the best she had ever created.

Three years later, Hinton's fans saw the fruits of her next attempt to extend herself as an artist in her collection of interwoven short stories called *Some of Tim's Stories*. These 14 stories explore the lives of two close cousins, Tim and Mike, whose fathers are both killed in a car accident when the boys are just teens. When the cousins are 25, Terry ends up in prison when a drug deal goes bad, but

Mike is able to get away, fleeing to live in Oklahoma as a bartender and bouncer.

The stories, none of which are longer than 1,000 words, go back and forth in time. "The Sweetest Sound" describes Mike at the age of nine waking up to the sound of his father, a Vietnam War veteran, crying out in his sleep from bad dreams; "Full Moon Birthday," on the other hand, looks at Mike's first legal drink and sexual encounter. Other stories look at Mike's occasionally dangerous work at the bar, as well as his attempts at befriending his pretty English instructor at the local college.

By the end of the collection, it is apparent that Tim, the narrator of these stories, is actually Mike, the hero of the stories. Like Ponyboy before him, Tim is attempting to make some sort of sense of his life by writing it down, by turning his experiences into art. Ponyboy, however, tells his own story directly. Tim is writing in the third person, creating a distance between himself and his creation.

Having that kind of distance between narrator and protagonist, Hinton is able to demonstrate how a writer—Tim—develops and is able use his own life to become another character—Mike. Writing in this way proved to be an interesting challenge for Hinton, as she explained to *Vanity Fair*, "Tim is the writer of the short stories, although he calls himself Mike. So I had to be Tim, who was writing about Mike. It was like doing a first-person narrative once removed. I still had to know everything about Tim, whether he wrote about it or not. The experience was as intense as any first-person narrative I've done."[8]

Indeed, writing the stories provided challenges that Hinton didn't imagine when she set out to work, "When I first started writing from Tim's point of view, I was amazed that I couldn't do dialogue, because dialogue is my strong point.

S.E. Hinton in 2007. Since its publication in 1967, The Outsiders *has sold more than 10 million copies. While she knows she will likely remain best known for that book, she has no plans to write a sequel. Instead, she looks forward to the challenges of writing new works for a variety of audiences—young children, teenagers, and adults.*

But dialogue was the hardest part of fiction writing for Tim. In the earlier stories there's not much. But as he got more relaxed with his writing, he got more comfortable doing dialogue as well."[9]

Hinton is extraordinarily proud of the collection, proclaiming in an interview that Tim's stories are "the best writing I've ever done. They may be the best writing I'll ever do. . . . I do think these stories are going to stand the test of time and will end up being mentioned as some of my best work."[10]

Unfortunately, *Some of Tim's Stories*, which was more experimental in tone and structure than her better-known earlier work, was printed by a small publisher, the University of Oklahoma Press, and did not garner nearly the attention it deserved. Also, when there were reviews, they were often unfavorable comparisons to her earlier work, as in these comments by Stephanie Zacharek in *The New York Times*:

> Even though these stories are admirably direct, they also feel truncated and at times incomplete. Suddenly the truth hits: What's missing is the swaggering dirty-dungaree dialogue of *The Outsiders* and the rambling yet weirdly concise interior monologues of Ponyboy, its confused but eminently likable narrator.

There's just no book like *The Outsiders*, and even Hinton seems to know it.[11]

LIVING IN THE SHADOW

Zacharek is correct: S.E. Hinton knows that she will likely remain best known for *The Outsiders*. It is still her most read and best loved book—even now, more than 40 years after its publication. (In 2001, according to *Publishers*

Weekly, it was second only to *Charlotte's Web* as the best-selling children's paperback book of all time, with nearly 10,000,000 copies sold. It still sells more than 500,000 copies a year.)

Though Hinton strongly believes that she is a better writer now than she was then, she has given up on the hope that she will write something equally as beloved. As she said in an interview, "How can you top something that has touched people the way *The Outsiders* has? I don't even worry about that."[12]

Of course, there *is* one question that her fans always ask—"Will you ever write a sequel to *The Outsiders*?"—to which her answer is a respectful "no." For Hinton, *The Outsiders* is what it is, complete and of itself. As she also points out, she is no longer 16 years old, and, though she remembers being that age well, she knows that she will never be able to capture that moment again in quite the same way. As a writer, Hinton is not looking back, but forward to new projects. (Hinton does add one caveat to her refusal to write a sequel to *The Outsiders*. She has said that she *may* write a sequel to be placed in a safe deposit box, to be published after her death, if only to keep another writer from trying to write a sequel.)

Of course, Hinton is grateful for the financial freedom that the success of *The Outsiders* has provided her and is touched by the letters that she receives from people who read the book when they were teenagers and are passing it along to their own children to read and enjoy. What writer wouldn't be happy with a legacy like that?

As her subsequent books have demonstrated, though, Hinton was not just a one-book novelist. The Best Books for Young Adults awards she received from 1967 to 1979, together with being the first recipient of the Margaret A.

Edwards Lifetime Achievement Award by the American Library Association's Young Adult Services Division and *School Library Journal* is proof of that. Although Hinton is not the most prolific of novelists, when she does write, it matters. Her achievements as a writer for young adults are second to none.

Sitting in front of her typewriter as a young girl, writing *The Outsiders* for her own pleasure, out of a basic need to tell the story of what she saw around her, Susie Hinton could not have imagined that she was opening the door to a whole new genre of young adult fiction. Thanks to her, today's young readers not only have Hinton's novels to read, but also hundreds of other fine books, none of which would have been as easily published without her trailblazing efforts. Hinton herself is proud of what she has accomplished and looks forward to continuing to explore her talents as a writer. "I was given a gift," she said in an interview. "It's my duty to use it in the best way I can. I don't want to throw it back in God's face. But the fact that I enjoy writing makes everything kind of easy."[13]

CHRONOLOGY

1950   July 22, Susan Eloise Hinton is born; some sources give her date of birth as 1948.

1965   Hinton, an aspiring writer, begins work on *The Outsiders*.

1966   Hinton graduates from Will Rogers High School in Tulsa, Oklahoma; on the same day, she receives a contract from Viking Press to publish *The Outsiders*; that fall, Hinton enters the University of Tulsa.

1967   *The Outsiders* is published to widespread acclaim; sales quickly pick up due to strong word-of-mouth response.

1968   Hinton's short story "Rumble Fish" is published in the literary supplement of the University of Tulsa Alumni Magazine, *Nimrod*.

1970   Hinton graduates from the University of Tulsa with a degree in education; marries longtime boyfriend David Inhofe; spends several months in Europe, mostly in Spain, on honeymoon.

1971   *That Was Then, This Is Now* is published.

1975   *Rumble Fish* is published.

1979   *Tex* is published.

1982   *Tex* is released as a feature film by Disney Films; Hinton helps the film's director, Tim Hunger, scout locations and select wardrobe, contributes a few lines of dialogue, and makes her acting debut in the film, playing a cameo role as the typing teacher.

1983   Film versions of *The Outsiders* and *Rumble Fish* are filmed in Tulsa, Oklahoma, both directed by Francis Ford Coppola; Hinton co-writes the films' screenplays, works closely with the cast of *The Outsiders*, and makes cameo appearances in both films.

1985   *That Was Then, This Is Now* is released as a feature film; Hinton has no involvement with the film's production.

1988   Hinton is awarded the first Margaret A. Edwards Lifetime Achievement Award by the American Library Association's Young Adult Services Division and *School Library Journal*, honoring her outstanding contribution to literature for young adults; *Taming the Star Runner* is published.

1995 Hinton writes two children's books: *Big David, Little David* and *The Puppy Sister*, which are published to mixed reviews.

1998 Hinton is inducted into the Oklahoma Writers Hall of Fame.

2004 Hinton's first "adult" book, *Hawkes Harbor*, is published to largely negative reviews.

2007 *The Outsiders* celebrates its fortieth anniversary of publication; Hinton's first collection of short stories, *Some of Tim's Stories*, is published.

NOTES

Chapter 1

1 S.E. Hinton, *Some of Tim's Stories*. Norman, Okla.: University of Oklahoma Press, 2007, p. 72.

2 Jay Daly, *Presenting S.E. Hinton*. New York: Dell, 1989, preface.

3 Lauren Sozio. "Some of Hinton's Stories." *Vanity Fair*, May 14, 2007. http://www.vanityfair.com/culture/features/2007/05/hinton qanda200705.

4 "Who says teens don't read?" *Roanoke Times*, October 23, 2007. http://www.roanoke.com/entertainment/wb/xp-136866.

5 "1988 Margaret A. Edwards Award Winner." Young Adult Library Services Association Web site. http://www.ala.org/ala/mgrps/divs/yalsa/booklistsawards/margaretaedwards/maeprevious/1988awardwinner.cfm.

Chapter 2

1 Daly, *Presenting S.E. Hinton*, p. 4.

2 S.E. Hinton, *Tex*. New York: Dell, 1983, p. 171.

3 Dinitia Smith. "An Outsider, Out of the Shadows." *New York Times*, September 7, 2005. http://www.nytimes.com/2005/09/07/movies/MoviesFeatures/07hint.html?_r=1&sq=An+Outsider%2C+Out+of+the+shadows&st=nyt&oref=slogin.

4 Hinton, *Some of Tim's Stories*, p. 96.

5 Daly, *Presenting S.E. Hinton*, p. 3.

6 Doris De Montreville and Elizabeth J. Crawford, eds., *Fourth Junior Book of Junior Authors*. New York: H.W. Wilson, 1978.

7 Lisa Ehrichs, "Advice from a Penwoman," *Seventeen*, Vol. 40, November 1981, p. 32.

8 Hinton, *Some of Tim's Stories*, pp. 73–74.

9 Smith, "An Outsider, Out of the Shadows," http://www.nytimes.com/2005/09/07/movies/MoviesFeatures/07/.hint.html?_r=1&sq=An+Outsider%2C+Out+of+the+Shadows&st=nyt&oref=slogin.

10 Ibid.

11 S.E. Hinton, *The Outsiders*. New York: Dell Publishing, 1983, p. 6.

12 Hinton, *Some of Tim's Stories*, p. 73.

13 Stephen Farber. "Directors Join the S.E. Hinton Fan Club." *New York Times*, March 20, 1983. http://select.nytimes.com/search/restricted/article?res=F40E1DFD3E5D0C738EDDAA0894DB484D81.

14 Hinton, *Some of Tim's Stories*, p. 74.

15 "S.E. Hinton and the ground-breaking 'Outsiders.'" CNN.com, October 4, 2007. http://www.cnn.com/2007/SHOWBIZ/books/10/03/books.se.hinton.ap/index.html.

16 Ehrichs, "Advice from a Penwoman."

17 Ibid.

18 Susan Hinton, "Teen-Agers Are for Real," *New York Times*, August 27, 1967. http://select.nytimes.com/gst/abstract.html?res=F10C15F93B5D10708DDDAE0A94D0405B878AF1D3&scp=1&sq=&st=p.

Chapter 3

1 Hinton, *Some of Tim's Stories*, p. 76.

2 Ibid., p. 77.

3 Ehrichs, "Advice from a Penwoman."

4 Hinton, *The Outsiders*, p. 14.

5 Ibid., p. 44.

6 Ibid., p. 69.

7 Ibid., p. 15.

8 Ibid., p. 155.

9 Ibid., p. 156.

10 "Biography of S.E. Hinton." *Encyclopedia of World Biography*. http://www.bookrags.com/biography/se-hinton-aya/.

11 Ibid.

12 Ibid.

13 Hinton, *Some of Tim's Stories*, p. 77.

14 Daly, *Presenting S.E. Hinton*, p. 16.

15 Hinton, *Some of Tim's Stories*, p. 82.

16 Ibid., p. 83.

17 "S.E. Hinton and the groundbreaking 'Outsiders,'" CNN.com, http://www.cnn.com/2007/SHOWBIZ/books/10/03/books.se.hinton.ap/index.html.

18 Ibid.

19 "Pony will always be gold." Amazon.com Review, May 1, 2008. http://www.amazon.com/review/product/014038572X/ref=cm_cr_dp_all_helpful?%5FEncoding=UTF8&coliid=%showViewpoints=1%colid=&sortBy+bySubmissionDateDescending.

Chapter 4

1 Daly, *Presenting S.E. Hinton*, p. 37.

2 Hinton, *Some of Tim's Stories*, p. 78.

3 Daly, *Presenting S.E. Hinton*, p. 79.

4 Hinton, *Some of Tim's Stories*, p. 90.

5 S.E. Hinton, *That Was Then, This Is Now*. New York: Dell, 1980, p. 5.

6 Jerry Weiss, ed., *From Writers to Students: The Pleasure and Pains of Writing*. Newark, Del.: International Reading Association, 1979, pp. 32–38.

7 Hinton, *That Was Then, This Is Now*, p. 61.

8 Ibid., p. 62.

9 Ibid., p. 153.

10 Ibid., p. 154.

11 Hinton, *Some of Tim's Stories*, p. 92.

12 Ibid.

13 Ibid., p. 94.

14 Daly, *Presenting S.E. Hinton*, p. 47.

15 "Biography S.E. Hinton," *Contemporary Authors*. Gale Reference Team, 2005.

Chapter 5

1 Hinton, *Some of Tim's Stories*, p. 95.

2 S.E. Hinton, *Rumble Fish*. New York: Dell, 1989, p. 115.

3 Ibid.

4 Hinton, *Some of Tim's Stories*, p. 95.

5 "Biography of S.E. Hinton." Book Rags. http://www.bookrags.com/biography/se-hinton-aya/.

6 Hinton, *Rumble Fish*, p. 6.

7 Ibid., p. 68.

8 Hinton, *Some of Tim's Stories*, p. 97.

9 Daly, *Presenting S.E. Hinton*, p. 66.

10 Ibid.

11 Jane Abramson, "Review of *Rumble Fish*," *School Library Journal*, November 1979, p. 106.

12 Daly, *Presenting S.E. Hinton*, p. 84.

13 Hinton, *Some of Tim's Stories*, pp. 97–98.

14 S.E. Hinton. "On Writing Tex." Delacorte Press's Notes from Delacorte Press. http://falcon.jmu.edu/~ramseyil/hinton.htm.

15 Ibid.

16 Hinton, *Some of Tim's Stories*, p. 98.

17 S.E. Hinton, *Tex*, p. 102.

18 Ibid., p. 105.

19 Hinton, "On Writing Tex," http://falcon.jmu.edu/~ramsey/11/hinton.htm.

20 Daly, *Presenting S.E. Hinton*, p. 97.

21 Hinton, *Tex*, pp. 110–111.

22 Marilyn Kaye, "Review of *Tex*," *School Library Journal*, November 15, 1979, p. 88.

23 Margery Fisher, "Review of *Tex*," *Growing Points*, May 1980, pp. 3686–3687.

24 Paxton Davis, "Review of *Tex*," *New York Times Book Review*, December 16, 1979, p. 23.

25 Lance Salway, "Review of *Tex*," *Signal*, May 1980, pp. 120–122.

Chapter 6

1 Farber, "Directors Join the S.E. Hinton Fan Club," http://select.nytimes.com/search/restricted/article?res=F40E1EFD3E5D0C738EDDAA0894DB484D81.

2 Hinton, *Some of Tim's Stories*, p. 109.

3 Farber, "Directors Join the S.E. Hinton Fan Club," http://select.nytimes.com/search/restricted/article?res=F40E1EFD3E5D0C738EDDAA0894DB484D81.

4 Hinton, *Some of Tim's Stories*, p. 110.

5 Farber, "Directors Join the S.E. Hinton Fan Club," http://select.nytimes.com/search/restricted/article?res=F40E1EFD3E5D0C738EDDAA0894DB484D81.

6 Hinton, *Some of Tim's Stories*, p. 111.

7 Farber, "Directors Join the S.E. Hinton Fan Club," http://select.nytimes.com/search/restricted/article?res=F40E1EFD3E5D0C738EDDAA0894DB484D81.

8 Ibid.

9 "S.E. Hinton and the groundbreaking 'Outsiders,'" http://www.cnn.com/2007/SHOWBIZ/books/10/03/books.se.hinton.ap/index.html.

10 Farber, "Directors Join the S.E. Hinton Fan Club," http://select.nytimes.com/search/restricted/article?res=F40E1EFD3E5D0C738EDDAA0894D484D81.

11 Ibid.

12 Ibid.

13 Hinton, *Some of Tim's Stories*, p. 115.

14 Ibid., p. 117.

15 Farber, "Directors Join the S.E. Hinton Fan Club," http://select. nytimes.com/search/restricted/ article?res=F40E1EFD3E5D0C738 EDDAA0894D484D81.

Chapter 7

1 Dave Smith, "Hinton, What Boys Are Made Of," *Los Angeles Times*, July 15, 1982, p. 27.

2 S.E. Hinton, *Taming the Star Runner*. New York: Dell, 1988, p. 1.

3 Hinton, *Some of Tim's Stories*, p. 102.

4 Sozzio, "Some of Hinton's Stories," http://www.vanityfair. com/culture/features/2007/05/ hintonqanda200705.

5 Hinton, *Taming the Star Runner*, p. 181.

6 Ibid., p. 9.

7 Ibid., p. 111.

8 Ibid., p. 112.

9 Hinton, *Some of Tim's Stories*, p. 101.

10 Nancy Vasilakis, "Review of *Taming the Star Runner*," *Horn Book*, Jan.–Feb. 1989, pp. 78–79.

11 Ibid.

12 Patty Campbell. "Review of *Taming the Star Runner*." *New York Times Book Review*, April 2, 1989. http://query.nytimes. com/gst/fullpage.html?res=950DE6 D61138F931A35757C0A96F94826 0&sec=&span=.

13 Ibid.

14 Daly, *Presenting S.E. Hinton*, pp. 126–128.

Chapter 8

1 Marylou Moreno Kjelle, *S.E. Hinton: Author of* The Outsiders. Berkeley Heights, N.J.: Enslow, 2008, p. 83.

2 Cindy Lynn Speer and Wiley Saichek. "An Interview with S.E. Hinton." Bookreporter.com, October 8, 2004. http://www.bookreporter. com/authors/au-hinton-se.asp.

3 Hinton, *Some of Tim's Stories*, pp. 124–125.

4 "Review of *The Puppy Sister*," *Publishers Weekly*, July 17, 1995, p. 37.

5 Hinton, *Some of Tim's Stories*, p. 131.

6 Speer and Saichek, "An Interview with S.E. Hinton," http://www. bookreporter.com/authors/au-hinton-se.asp.

7 Elizabeth Hand, "The Lost Boys," *Washington Post*, December 12, 2004, p. T05.

8 Sozio, "Some of Hinton's Stories," http://www.vanityfair.com/culture/ features/2007/05/hintonqanda 200705.

9 Hinton, *Some of Tim's Stories*, p. 140.

10 Ibid., p. 148.

11 Stephanie Zacharek. "Adult Themes." *New York Times Book Review*, May 13, 2007. http://www. nytimes.com/2007/05/13/books/ review/Zacharek-t.html?ref=books.

12 Hinton, *Some of Tim's Stories*, p. 91.

13 Ibid., p. 150.

WORKS BY S.E. HINTON

1967 *The Outsiders*
1971 *That Was Then, This Is Now*
1975 *Rumble Fish*
1979 *Tex*
1988 *Taming the Star Runner*
1995 *Big David, Little David*
1995 *The Puppy Sister*
2004 *Hawkes Harbor*
2007 *Some of Tim's Stories*

POPULAR BOOKS

THE OUTSIDERS

The story of teenage gangs and restless disaffected youth in Tulsa, Oklahoma, *The Outsiders* remains Hinton's most popular and beloved novel. Written when she was just 16, it forever changed the world of young adult literature.

RUMBLE FISH

Rusty-James wants to be just like his older brother, the mysterious Motorcycle Boy. He soon learns, however, that heroes aren't always what they appear to be.

TAMING THE STAR RUNNER

Travis, a cool city guy, is sent to live on his uncle's ranch in an effort to keep him out of trouble. While there, he falls in love with Casey, a horse trainer attempting to tame the horse Star Runner, and learns where his true talents lie.

TEX

Fifteen-year-old Tex is charming, easy-going, and innocent. But a series of unfortunate incidents, including losing his beloved horse, Negrito, and a chance encounter with a dangerous stranger, force him to reevaluate his life.

THAT WAS THEN, THIS IS NOW

Bryon and Mark have been best friends since childhood. But now, at the age of 16, drugs and violence begin to drive them apart.

POPULAR CHARACTERS

CASEY

The strongest of Hinton's female characters, Casey Kincaide is training riders for an upcoming horse show, while working with her own horse, the untamed Star Runner. Like Travis, she too is an artist, but has a discipline that Travis lacks.

MOTORCYCLE BOY

A former gang leader and older brother of Rusty-James, Motorcycle Boy is described as a "perfect knight." Unfortunately for him, he was born in the wrong place and time and can find nothing that he wants to do or that will give his life meaning.

PONYBOY CURTIS

More than 40 years after the publication of *The Outsiders*, Ponyboy remains Hinton's most popular character. Though a greaser on the outside, inside he remains sensitive, literate, and hopeful for something better as he, his brothers, and his friends navigate a world divided between greasers and Socs.

RUSTY-JAMES

The hero of *Rumble Fish*, Rusty-James is a tough, not terribly intelligent or articulate, but basically innocent kid from the wrong side of town. He wants nothing more than to be like his idolized older brother, Motorcycle Boy, and to live in what he sees as the "good old days" of street gangs.

TEX

S.E. Hinton's "favorite child," Tex McCormack is open and honest. If he's not the toughest of Hinton's male protagonists, he's definitely the strongest. His innocence, sweetness, generous spirit, and sense of hopefulness makes him the most loveable, and perhaps the most completely human, of Hinton's characters.

TRAVIS

The hero of *Taming the Star Runner*, 15-year-old Travis Harris is a city boy trying to fit into rural life on his uncle's ranch. There he meets Casey, a tough, disciplined horse trainer working with the mysterious horse Star Runner. Travis, like Hinton herself, is an aspiring writer whose first book has been accepted for publication.

MAJOR AWARDS

1967 *The Outsiders* is ranked on the *New York Herald Tribune*'s Best Teenage Books list; *The Outsiders* is named as a *Chicago Tribune* "Book World" Spring Book Festival Honor Book.

1971 *That Was Then, This Is Now* is named to the American Library Association (ALA) Best Books for Young Adults list; *That Was Then, This Is Now* is named as a *Chicago Tribune* "Book World" Spring Book Festival Honor Book.

1975 *The Outsiders* wins the Media and Methods Maxi Award; *The Outsiders* is named to the ALA Best Books for Young Adults list; *Rumble Fish* is named to the ALA Best Books for Young Adults list; *Rumble Fish* is ranked as one of *School Library Journal*'s Best Books of the Year.

1978 *That Was Then, This Is Now* wins the Massachusetts Children's Book Award.

1979 *The Outsiders* wins the Massachusetts Children's Book Award; *Tex* is named to the ALA Best Books for Young Adults list; *Tex* is ranked as one of *School Library Journal*'s Best Books of the Year.

1980 *Tex* earns the New York Public Library "Book for the Teen-Age" citation.

1981 *Tex* receives an American Book Award nomination.

1982 *Rumble Fish* is presented with the New Mexico Library Association "Land of Enchantment" Book Award.

1988 *Taming the Star Runner* is named to the ALA Best Book for Young Adults list; Hinton wins the Margaret A. Edwards Award for "outstanding contribution to literature for young adults."

BIBLIOGRAPHY

BOOKS

Daly, Jay. *Presenting S.E. Hinton*. New York: Dell, 1989.

De Montreville, Doris, and Elizabeth Crawford, eds. *Fourth Book of Junior Authors*. New York: H.W. Wilson, 1978.

Hinton, S.E. *The Outsiders*. New York: Dell, 1983.

———. *Rumble Fish*. New York: Dell, 1989.

———. *Some of Tim's Stories*. Norman, Okla.: University of Oklahoma Press, 2007.

———. *Taming the Star Runner*. New York: Dell, 1989.

———. *Tex*. New York: Dell, 1983.

———. *That Was Then, This Is Now*. New York: Dell, 1980.

Kjelle, Marylou Morano. *S.E. Hinton: Author of* The Outsiders. Berkeley Heights, N.J.: Enslow, 2008.

PERIODICALS

Abramson, Jane. "Review of *Rumble Fish*." *School Library Journal*, November 1979, p. 106.

Campbell, Patty. "Review of *Taming the Star Runner*." *New York Times*, April 2, 1989. Available online. URL: http://query.nytimes.com/gst/fullpage.html?res=950DE6D61138F931A35757C0A96F948260&scp=1&sq=Taming+the+Star+Runner&st=nyt.

Davis, Paxton. "Review of *Tex*." *New York Times Book Review*, December 16, 1979, p. 23.

Ehrichs, Lisa. "Advice from a Penwoman." *Seventeen*, Vol. 40, November 1981, p. 32.

Farber, Stephen. "Directors Join the S.E. Hinton Fan Club." *New York Times*, March 20, 1983. Available online. URL: http://select.nytimes.com/search/restricted/article?res=F40E1EFD3E5D0C738EDDAA00894DB484D81.

Fisher, Margery. "Review of *Rumble Fish*." *Growing Point*, May 1976. Quoted in *Contemporary Authors Online*.

Hand, Elizabeth. "The Lost Boys." *Washington Post*, December 12, 2004.

Heater, Brian. "Staying Golden." *New York Press*, September 21, 2004. Available online. URL: http://www.nypress.com/print.cfm?content_id=11160.

Hinton, Susan. "Teen-Agers Are for Real." *New York Times*, August 27, 1967.

King, Marilyn, "Review of *Tex*," *School Library Journal*. Available online. URL: http://www.bookrags.com/biography/s-e-hinton-aya/.

Publishers Weekly. "Review of *The Puppy Sister*," Amazon.com. Available online. URL: http://www.amazon.com/Puppy-Sister-S-E-Hinton/dp/0440413842/refpd_bbs_sr_1&ie=UTF8&s=books&qid=1211310451&sr=1-1.

Salway, Lance. "Review of *Tex*." *Signal*, May 1980. Available online. URL: http://www.bookrags.com/biography/susan-eloise-hinton/.

Smith, Dave. "Hinton, What Boys Are Made Of." *Los Angeles Times*, July 15, 1982.

Smith, Dinitia. "An Outsider, Out of the Shadows." *New York Times*, September 7, 2005. Available online. URL: http://www.nytimes.com/2005/09/07/movies/MoviesFeatures/07.hint.html?-r=1&sq=An=Outsider%2C+Out+of+the+Shadows&st=nyt&oref=slogin.

Sozio, Lauren. "Some of Hinton's Stories." *Vanity Fair*, May 14, 2007. Available online. URL: http://www.vanityfair.com/culture/features/2007/05/hinstonqanda200705.

Vasilakis, Nancy. "Review of *Taming the Star Runner*." *Horn Book*, January–February 1989.

Walsh, William. "S.E. Hinton." *From Writers to Students: The Pleasures and Pains of Writing*. Edited by M. Jerry Weiss. Newark, Del.: International Reading Association, 1977.

"Who says teens don't read?" *Roanoke Times*, October 23, 2007. Available online. URL: http://www.roanoke.com/entertainment/wb/xp-136866.

Zacharek, Stephanie. "Adult Themes." *New York Times*, May 13, 2007. Available online. URL: http://www.nytimes.com/2007/05/13/books/review/Zacharek-t.html?ref=books.

OTHER SOURCES

"1988 Margaret A. Edwards Award Winner." Young Adult Library Services Association. Available online. URL: http://www.ala.org/ala/mgrps/divs/yalsa/booklistsawards/margaretedwards/maeprevious/1988awardwinner.cfm.

"Biography of S.E. Hinton." *Encyclopedia of World Biography*. Available online. URL: http://www.bookrags.com/biography/s-e-hinton-aya/.

"Biography of S.E. Hinton." Available online. URL: http://www.bookrags. com/biography/susan-eloise-hinston-dtx/.

Hinton, S.E., "On Writing Tex." Delacorte Press's Notes from Delacorte Press. Available online. URL: http://falcon.jum.edu/~ramseyil/hinton. htm.

"Pony will always be gold." Review posted on Amazon.com, May 1, 2008. Available online. URL: http://www.amazon.com/review/ product/015038572X/ref=cm_cr_dp_all_helpful?%5Fencoding=UTF8 &coliid=&showViewpoints=1&colid=&sortBy=bySubmissionDateD escending.

"S.E. Hinton and the groundbreaking 'Outsiders.'" CNN.com, October 4, 2007. Available online. URL: http://www.cnn.com/2007/SHOWBIZ/ books/10/03/books.se.hinton.ap/index.html.

Speer, Cindy Lynn, and Wiley Saichek, "An Interview with S.E. Hinton." Bookreporter. Available online. URL: http://www.bookreporter.com/ authors/au=hinton-se.asp.

FURTHER READING

Bergan, Ronald. *Francis Ford Coppola Close Up: The Making of His Movies*. New York: Thunder's Mouth Press, 1998.

Cleary, Beverly. *Fifteen*. New York: HarperTrophy, 1996.

Frost, Robert. *The Poetry of Robert Frost*. New York: Holt Paperbacks, 2002.

Henry, Marguerite. *King of the Wind: The Story of the Godolphin Arabian*. New York: Simon & Schuster, 2006.

Jackson, Shirley. *The Haunting of Hill House*. New York: Penguin Classics, 2006.

Mitchell, Margaret. *Gone with the Wind*. New York: Scribner, 2007.

Seton, Ernest Thompson. *Wild Animals I Have Known*. Chapel Hill, N.C.: Yesterday's Classics, 2007.

PICTURE CREDITS

INDEX

ABOUT THE CONTRIBUTOR

DENNIS ABRAMS is the author of several books, including biographies of Barbara Park, Anthony Horowitz, Hamid Karzai, and Ty Cobb for Chelsea House. He attended Antioch College, where he majored in English and communications. He currently lives in Houston, Texas.